greatest ever

baking

p

This is a Parragon Book
This edition published in 2002

Parragon
Queen Street House
4 Queen Street
Bath BA1 1HE, UK

ISBN: 0-75259-455-9

Printed in Dubai

Produced by the Bridgewater Book Company Ltd

NOTE

This book uses metric and imperial measurements. Follow the same units
of measurement throughout; do not mix metric and imperial.
All spoon measurements are level: teaspoons are assumed to be 5 ml,
and tablespoons are assumed to be 15 ml. Unless otherwise stated,
milk is assumed to be full fat, eggs and individual vegetables such as potatoes
are medium, and pepper is freshly ground black pepper.

The times given for each recipe are an approximate guide only because the
preparation times may differ according to the techniques used by different
people and the cooking times may vary as a result of the type of oven used.

Recipes using raw or very lightly cooked eggs should be
avoided by infants, the elderly, pregnant women, convalescents, and anyone
suffering from an illness.

Contents

Introduction

It may be a daunting prospect to bake your own bread, pastries, biscuits and cakes instead of buying them ready-made at the supermarket, but once you have acquired the basic skills – and armed yourself with a few of the 'tricks' – it becomes fun, versatile and rewarding.

There are a few points that will ensure your baking session is successful, regardless of the type of recipe you have chosen. So, before you start:

- Read through the recipe carefully, and make sure you have the right ingredients – using plain flour when self-raising flour is specified, for example, may not produce the result you were expecting!
- Remember to preheat the oven to the right temperature.
- Make sure you are using the correct size and shape of tin or dish because the quantities given in the recipe are for the size of the tin specified.
- Prepare the cookware before you start assembling any of the ingredients – grease or line tins, dishes or baking sheets as directed in the recipe.
- Weigh all the ingredients accurately, and do any basic preparation, such as chopping, slicing or grating, before you start cooking.
- Once you start cooking, follow the recipe step-by-step, in the order given. Using high-quality ingredients will give the best results – unbleached flours and unrefined sugars are readily available and are best for cakes; fresh vegetables, fish and meat from a reliable supplier, and a good, extra virgin olive oil will make all the difference to savoury bakes.

Pastry

- Metal tins, rather than porcelain dishes, are best for quiches and tarts.
- Use fat at room temperature, cut into small pieces.
- Use ice-cold water for mixing.
- Pastry benefits from cool ingredients and cold hands.
- Sieve dry ingredients into a mixing bowl to incorporate air.
- Wrap pastry in foil or clingfilm and allow it to 'rest' in the refrigerator for 30 minutes before using.

Bread

- Plan ahead – most bread recipes include one or two periods of 'proving' (leaving the dough in a warm place to double its bulk).
- If the flour feels cool, warm it gently in an oven at a low temperature before using.
- Make sure the liquid is hand-hot to activate the yeast.
- To knead dough, stretch it away from you with one hand while pulling it towards you with the other, then fold in the edges, give it a quarter turn, and repeat.
- To test whether bread is cooked, tap the base – it should sound hollow.

Cakes

- Using a loose-based tin will make it much easier to turn out the cake.
- Bring all the ingredients to room temperature before starting to bake.
- If possible, use a hand-held electric mixer for 'creaming' (beating together the butter and sugar until the mixture has a 'soft dropping' consistency).
- Fold in dry ingredients very gently, using a metal spoon or spatula in a figure-of-eight movement. This lets the air get to the mixture and stops the cake becoming too heavy.
- When the cake is cooked, it should feel springy when pressed lightly. Alternatively, insert a fine metal skewer into the centre of the cake – if it is cooked, the skewer should come out clean.

Basic Recipes

Ragù Sauce

MAKES ABOUT 600 ML/1 PINT

3 tbsp olive oil

3 tbsp butter

2 large onions, chopped

4 celery sticks, sliced thinly

175 g/6 oz streaky bacon, chopped

2 garlic cloves, chopped

500 g/1 lb 2 oz minced beef

2 tbsp tomato purée

1 tbsp plain flour

400 g/14 oz canned chopped tomatoes

150 ml/5 fl oz beef stock

150 ml/5 fl oz red wine

2 tsp dried oregano

½ tsp freshly grated nutmeg

salt and pepper

1 Heat the oil and butter in a pan over a medium heat. Add the onions, celery and bacon and fry for 5 minutes, stirring constantly.

2 Stir in the garlic and beef and cook, stirring, until the meat has lost its redness. Reduce the heat and simmer the mixture for 10 minutes, stirring occasionally.

3 Increase the heat to medium, stir in the tomato purée and the flour and cook for 1–2 minutes. Add the tomatoes, stock and wine and bring to the boil, stirring constantly. Season to taste, then stir in the oregano and nutmeg. Reduce the heat, then cover and simmer for 45 minutes, stirring occasionally. The sauce is now ready to use.

Basic Pizza Dough

MAKES ONE 25-CM/10-INCH PIZZA

175 g/6 oz plain flour, plus extra
   for dusting

1 tsp salt

1 tsp easy-blend dried yeast

6 tbsp hand-hot water

1 tbsp olive oil

1 Sieve the flour and salt into a large bowl and add the yeast. Pour in the water and oil and bring together to form a dough. Knead for 5 minutes, then leave in a warm place to rise until doubled in size.

2 Knock out the air from the dough, then knead lightly. Roll out on a lightly floured work surface, ready for use.

Fresh Vegetable Stock

This can be kept chilled for up to three days or frozen for up to three months. Salt is not added when cooking the stock: it is better to season it according to the dish in which it is to be used.

MAKES ABOUT 1.5 LITRES/2¾ PINTS

250 g/9 oz shallots

1 large carrot, diced

1 celery stick, chopped

½ fennel bulb

1 garlic clove

1 bay leaf

a few fresh parsley and
   tarragon sprigs

2 litres/ 3½ pints water

pepper

1 Place all the ingredients in a large pan and bring to the boil.

2 Skim off the surface scum with a flat spoon and reduce to a gentle simmer. Partially cover and cook for 45 minutes. Leave to cool.

3 Line a sieve with clean muslin and place over a large jug or bowl. Pour the stock through the sieve to strain, then discard the herbs and vegetables.

4 Cover and store in small quantities in the refrigerator for up to 3 days.

Pesto Sauce

MAKES ABOUT 300 ML/10 FL OZ

55 g/2 oz fresh parsley, chopped finely

2 garlic cloves, crushed

55 g/2 oz pine kernels, crushed

2 tbsp chopped fresh basil leaves

55 g/2 oz freshly grated
   Parmesan cheese

150 ml/5 fl oz olive oil

white pepper

1 Place all the ingredients in a food processor and process for 2 minutes. Alternatively, you can blend by hand using a pestle and mortar.

2 Season with white pepper, then transfer to a jug, cover with clingfilm and store in the refrigerator before using.

Desserts

Confirmed pudding lovers feel a meal is lacking

if there isn't a tempting dessert to finish off the

menu. Yet it is often possible to combine

indulgence with healthy ingredients. A lot of the recipes in this chapter contain

fruit, which is the perfect ingredient for healthy desserts that are still deliciously

tempting, such as Blackberry Pudding, Raspberry Shortcake, Paper-thin Fruit

Pies, Apple Tart Tatin and Baked Bananas. Some desserts are also packed full

of protein-rich nuts, such as Pine Kernel Tart and Almond Cheesecakes.

queen of puddings

serves eight

2 tbsp butter, plus extra for greasing

600 ml/1 pint milk

225 g/8 oz caster sugar

finely grated rind of 1 orange

4 eggs, separated

75 g/2¾ oz fresh breadcrumbs

pinch of salt

6 tbsp orange marmalade

COOK'S TIP

If you prefer a crisper meringue, bake the pudding in the oven for an extra 5 minutes.

VARIATION

Substitute the same quantity of fine sponge cake crumbs for the breadcrumbs and use raspberry, strawberry or apricot jam instead of orange marmalade.

1 Grease a 1.5-litre/2¾-pint ovenproof dish with butter.

2 To make the custard, heat the milk in a saucepan with the butter, 50 g/1¾ oz of the caster sugar and the grated orange rind until just warm.

3 Whisk the egg yolks in a bowl. Gradually pour the warm milk over the eggs, whisking constantly.

4 Stir the breadcrumbs into the saucepan, then transfer the mixture to the prepared dish and leave to stand for 15 minutes.

5 Bake in a preheated oven, 180°C/350°F/Gas Mark 4, for 20–25 minutes, until the custard has just set. Remove the custard from the oven, but do not turn the oven off.

6 To make the meringue, whisk the egg whites with the salt until they stand in soft peaks. Whisk in the remaining sugar, a little at a time.

7 Spread the orange marmalade over the cooked custard. Top with the meringue, spreading it right to the edges of the dish.

8 Return the pudding to the oven and bake for a further 20 minutes, until the meringue is crisp and golden. Serve immediately.

bread & butter pudding

serves six

5 tbsp butter, softened

4–5 slices of white or brown bread

4 tbsp chunky orange marmalade

grated rind of 1 lemon

85–125 g/3–4½ oz raisins
   or sultanas

40 g/1½ oz chopped mixed peel

1 tsp ground cinnamon or
   mixed spice

1 cooking apple, peeled, cored and
   roughly grated

85 g/3 oz light brown sugar

3 eggs

500 ml/18 fl oz milk

2 tbsp demerara sugar

1 Use the butter to grease an ovenproof dish generously and to spread on one side of each of the slices of bread, then spread the bread with the marmalade.

2 Place a layer of bread in the base of the prepared dish and sprinkle with the grated lemon rind, half of the raisins or sultanas, half of the mixed peel, half of the cinnamon or mixed spice, all of the apple and half of the light brown sugar.

3 Add another layer of bread, cutting the slices so that they fit the dish.

4 Sprinkle over most of the remaining raisins or sultanas and the remaining peel, spice and light brown sugar, sprinkling it evenly over the bread. Top with a final layer of bread, again cutting to fit the dish.

5 Lightly beat the eggs and milk together in a large mixing bowl, then carefully strain the mixture over the bread pudding in the ovenproof dish. If time allows, leave to stand for 20–30 minutes.

6 Sprinkle the top of the bread pudding with the demerara sugar and scatter over the remaining raisins or sultanas. Cook in a preheated oven, 200°C/400°F/Gas Mark 6, for 50–60 minutes, until risen and golden brown. Serve immediately if serving hot or leave to cool completely, then serve cold.

eve's pudding

COOK'S TIP

To increase the almond flavour,
add 25 g/1 oz ground almonds
with the flour in step 4.

1 Grease an 900-ml/1½-pint
ovenproof dish with butter.

2 Mix the apples with the lemon
juice, granulated sugar and
sultanas. Spoon into the prepared dish.

3 In a bowl, cream the butter and
caster sugar together until pale.
Add the egg, a little at a time.

4 Carefully fold in the self-raising
flour and stir in the milk to give
a soft, dropping consistency.

5 Spread the mixture over the
apples and sprinkle with the
flaked almonds.

6 Bake in a preheated oven, 180°C/
350°F/Gas Mark 4, for about
40–45 minutes. until the sponge is
golden brown.

7 Serve the pudding piping hot,
accompanied by home-made
custard or double cream.

raspberry shortcake

100 g/3½ oz butter, diced, plus
    extra for greasing

175 g/6 oz self-raising flour, plus
    extra for dusting

75 g/2¾ oz caster sugar

1 egg yolk

1 tbsp rose water

600 ml/1 pint whipping cream,
    whipped lightly

225 g/8 oz raspberries, plus a few
    extra for decoration

TO DECORATE

icing sugar

fresh mint leaves (optional)

COOK'S TIP

The shortcake can be made a few days in advance and stored in an airtight container until required.

VARIATION

This shortcake is equally delicious made with strawberries or stoned and sliced peaches, instead of raspberries.

1 Lightly grease 2 baking trays with a little butter.

2 To make the shortcake, sieve the flour into a bowl.

3 Rub the butter into the flour with your fingertips until the mixture resembles breadcrumbs.

4 Stir the sugar, egg yolk and rose water into the mixture and bring together with your fingers to form a soft dough. Divide the dough in half.

5 Roll each piece of dough into a 20-cm/8-inch round on a lightly floured surface. Carefully lift each one with the rolling pin on to the prepared baking tray, then crimp the edges of the dough.

6 Bake the shortcake in a preheated oven, 190°C/375°F/Gas Mark 5, for 15 minutes, until lightly golden brown. Transfer the shortcakes to a wire rack and leave to cool completely.

7 Mix the whipped cream with the raspberries, spoon the mixture on top of one of the shortcakes and spread it out evenly. Top with the other shortcake round, dust with icing sugar and decorate with the extra raspberries and mint leaves, if you wish.

plum cobbler

serves six

75 g/2¾ oz butter, melted and
   cooled, plus extra for greasing
1 kg/2 lb 4 oz plums, stoned
   and sliced
100 g/3½ oz caster sugar
1 tbsp lemon juice
250 g/9 oz plain flour
2 tsp baking powder
75 g/2¾ oz granulated sugar
1 egg, beaten
150 ml/5 fl oz buttermilk
double cream, to serve

1 Lightly grease a 2-litre/3½-pint
ovenproof dish with butter.

2 Gently mix the sliced plums,
caster sugar, lemon juice and
25 g/1 oz of the plain flour together
in a large bowl.

3 Spoon the coated plums into the
bottom of the prepared ovenproof
dish, spreading them out evenly.

4 Sift the remaining flour and
the baking powder into a large
bowl and add the granulated sugar.
Stir well to mix.

5 Add the beaten egg, buttermilk
and cooled melted butter. Mix
everything gently together to form a
soft dough.

6 Place spoonfuls of the dough on
top of the fruit mixture until it is
almost completely covered.

7 Bake the cobbler in a preheated
oven, 190°C/375°F/Gas Mark 5,
for about 35–40 minutes, until the
topping is golden brown and the fruit
mixture is bubbling.

8 Serve the pudding piping hot,
with double cream.

3

5

6

blackberry pudding

serves four

6 tbsp butter, melted, plus extra
  for greasing

450 g/1 lb blackberries

75 g/2¾ oz caster sugar

1 egg

75 g/2¾ oz soft brown sugar, plus
  extra for sprinkling

8 tbsp milk

125 g/4½ oz self-raising flour

1 Lightly grease a 900-ml/1½-pint
  ovenproof dish with butter.

2 Gently mix the blackberries and
  caster sugar together in a large
mixing bowl until well blended.

3 Transfer the blackberry and sugar
  mixture to the prepared dish.

4 In a separate bowl, beat the egg
  and soft brown sugar together.
Stir in the melted butter and milk.

VARIATION

You can add 2 tablespoons of
cocoa powder to the batter in
step 5, if you like.

5 Sieve the flour into the egg and
  butter mixture and fold together
lightly with a figure-of-eight movement
to form a smooth batter.

6 Carefully spread the batter over
  the blackberry and sugar mixture
in the ovenproof dish.

7 Bake the pudding in a preheated
  oven, 180°C/350°F/Gas Mark 4,
for about 25–30 minutes, until the
topping is firm and golden.

8 Sprinkle the pudding with a little
  soft brown sugar and serve hot.

treacle tart

serves eight

250 g/9 oz shortcrust pastry dough,
   thawed if frozen

plain flour, for dusting

350 g/12 oz golden syrup

125 g/4½ oz fresh white
   breadcrumbs

125 ml/4 fl oz double cream

finely grated rind of ½ lemon
   or orange

2 tbsp lemon or orange juice

home-made custard, to serve

COOK'S TIP

Syrup is notoriously sticky and so can be quite difficult to measure. Dip the spoon in hot water first and the syrup will slide off it more easily and completely.

VARIATION

Use the pastry trimmings to create a lattice pattern on top of the tart, if you wish.

1 Roll out the pastry on a lightly floured work surface and use it to line a 20-cm/8-inch loose-bottomed quiche or flan tin, reserving the pastry trimmings. Prick the base of the pastry with a fork and leave to chill in the refrigerator for 30 minutes.

2 Cut out small shapes from the reserved pastry trimmings, such as leaves, stars or hearts, to decorate the top of the tart.

3 Mix the syrup, breadcrumbs, double cream, grated lemon or orange rind and lemon or orange juice together in a bowl.

4 Pour the mixture into the pastry case and decorate the edges of the tart with the pastry cut-outs.

5 Bake in a preheated oven, 190°C/ 375°F/Gas Mark 5 for about 35–40 minutes, or until the filling is just set.

6 Leave the tart to cool slightly in the tin. Turn out and serve warm with home-made custard.

apple tart tatin

serves eight

125 g/4½ oz butter

125 g/4½ oz caster sugar

4 eating apples, cored and quartered

250 g/9 oz shortcrust pastry dough,
   thawed if frozen

plain flour, for dusting

crème fraîche, to serve

1 Heat the butter and sugar in a 23-cm/9-inch ovenproof frying pan over a medium heat for about 5 minutes, until the mixture is just starting to caramelize. Remove the frying pan from the heat.

2 Arrange the apple quarters, skin side down, in the frying pan, taking care as the butter and sugar will be very hot. Place the frying pan back on the heat and simmer for 2 minutes.

3 Roll out the pastry on a lightly floured surface to form a circle just a little larger than the frying pan.

4 Place the pastry over the apples, press down and carefully tuck in the edges to seal the apples under the layer of pastry.

5 Bake the tart in a preheated oven, 200°C/400°F/Gas Mark 6 for 20–25 minutes, until the pastry is golden. Remove from the oven and leave to cool for about 10 minutes.

6 Place a serving plate over the frying pan and invert so that the pastry forms the base of the turned-out tart. Serve warm with crème fraîche.

fruit crumble tart

serves eight

PASTRY

150 g/5½ oz plain flour, plus extra
　for dusting

25 g/1 oz caster sugar

125 g/4½ oz butter, diced

1 tbsp water

FILLING

250 g/9 oz raspberries

450 g/1 lb plums, halved, stoned
　and roughly chopped

3 tbsp demerara sugar

CRUMBLE TOPPING

125 g/4½ oz plain flour

75 g/2¾ oz demerara sugar

100 g/3½ oz butter, diced

100 g/3½ oz chopped mixed nuts

1 tsp ground cinnamon

single cream or ice cream,
　to serve

1 To make the pastry, place the plain flour, sugar and butter in a bowl and rub in the butter with your fingertips until the mixture resembles breadcrumbs. Add the water and bring together with your fingers to form a soft dough. Wrap the dough in clingfilm and chill in the refrigerator for 30 minutes.

2 Roll out the pastry on a lightly floured work surface and use it to line the base of a 24-cm/9½-inch loose-bottomed quiche or flan tin. Prick the pastry with a fork and chill in the refrigerator for about 30 minutes.

3 To make the filling, toss the raspberries and plums together with the sugar and spoon into the pastry case.

4 To make the crumble topping, mix the flour, sugar and butter together in a bowl. Rub in the butter with your fingertips until the mixture resembles breadcrumbs. Stir in the nuts and ground cinnamon.

5 Sprinkle the topping over the fruit and press down gently with the back of a spoon. Bake in a preheated oven, 200°C/400°F/Gas Mark 6, for 20–25 minutes, until the topping is golden brown. Serve the tart with single cream or ice cream.

paper-thin fruit pies

serves four

1 eating apple

1 ripe pear

2 tbsp lemon juice

55 g/2 oz low-fat spread

4 sheets of filo pastry, thawed
   if frozen

2 tbsp low-sugar apricot jam

1 tbsp unsweetened orange juice

1 tbsp finely chopped pistachio nuts

2 tsp icing sugar, for dusting

low-fat custard, to serve

COOK'S TIP

Keep the unused sheets of filo
pastry covered with a clean,
damp tea towel until you are
ready to use them, as they dry
out easily.

VARIATION

Other combinations of fruit are
equally delicious. Try peach and
apricot, raspberry and apple or
pineapple and mango.

1 Core and thinly slice the apple
and pear and toss them in the
lemon juice.

2 Melt the low-fat spread in a small
saucepan over a low heat. Cut
each sheet of pastry into 4 and cover
with a clean, damp tea towel. Brush
4 non-stick Yorkshire pudding tins,
10 cm/4 inches wide, with a little of
the melted low-fat spread.

3 Working on each pie separately,
brush 4 sheets of pastry with low-
fat spread. Press a small sheet of pastry
into the base of 1 tin. Arrange the
other sheets of pastry on top at slightly
different angles. Repeat with the
remaining sheets of pastry to make
another 3 pies.

4 Arrange the apple and pear slices
alternately in the centre of each
pastry case and lightly crimp the
edges of the pastry of each fruit pie.

5 Mix the jam and orange juice
together until smooth and brush
over the fruit. Bake in a preheated
oven, 200°C/400°F/Gas Mark 6, for
12–15 minutes.

6 Sprinkle with the pistachio nuts,
dust lightly with icing sugar and
serve hot with low-fat custard.

custard tart

serves eight

PASTRY

150 g/5½ oz plain flour, plus extra
for dusting

25 g/1 oz caster sugar

125 g/4½ oz butter, diced

1 tbsp water

FILLING

3 eggs

150 ml/5 fl oz single cream

150 ml/5 fl oz milk

freshly grated nutmeg

1 To make the pastry, place the flour and sugar in a bowl and rub in the butter with your fingertips until the mixture resembles breadcrumbs.

2 Add the water and bring together with your fingers to form a soft dough. Wrap in clingfilm and chill in the refrigerator for about 30 minutes.

3 Roll out the dough on a lightly floured surface and use to line a 24-cm/9½-inch loose-bottomed quiche or flan tin.

4 Trim the edges of the pastry case, prick the base with a fork and chill in the refrigerator for 30 minutes.

5 Line the pastry case with foil and baking beans.

6 Bake the case in a preheated oven, 190°C/375°F/Gas Mark 5, for 15 minutes. Remove the foil and beans and bake for 15 minutes more.

7 To make the filling, whisk the eggs, cream, milk and nutmeg together. Pour into the prepared pastry case. Return the tart to the oven and cook for 25–30 minutes, or until just set, then serve.

4

7

baked sweet ravioli

SWEET PASTA DOUGH

425 g/15 oz plain flour, plus extra
  for dusting
140 g/5 oz butter, plus extra
  for greasing
140 g/5 oz caster sugar
4 eggs
25 g/1 oz yeast
125 ml/4 fl oz hand-hot milk

FILLING

175 g/6 oz chestnut purée
55 g/2 oz cocoa powder
55 g/2 oz caster sugar
55 g/2 oz chopped almonds
55 g/2 oz crushed amaretti biscuits
175 g/6 oz orange marmalade

1 To make the sweet pasta dough, sieve the flour into a large mixing bowl, then mix in the butter, sugar and 3 of the eggs.

2 Mix the yeast and warm milk together in a small bowl and when thoroughly blended, mix into the dough.

3 Knead the dough for 20 minutes, cover with a clean cloth and leave in a warm place for 1 hour to rise.

4 In a separate bowl, mix the chestnut purée, cocoa, sugar, almonds, crushed amaretti biscuits and orange marmalade together.

5 Generously grease a large baking tray with some butter.

6 Roll out the sweet dough into a thin sheet on a lightly floured work surface. Cut into 5-cm/2-inch rounds with a plain pastry cutter.

7 Put a spoonful of filling on to one half of each pasta round, then fold in half, pressing the edges firmly together to seal. Transfer the ravioli to the prepared baking tray, spacing them out well. Bake in batches, if necessary.

8 Beat the remaining egg and brush over the ravioli to glaze. Bake in a preheated oven, 180°C/350°F/Gas Mark 4, for 20 minutes. Serve hot.

lemon tart

serves eight

PASTRY

150 g/5½ oz plain flour, plus extra
    for dusting

25 g/1 oz caster sugar

125 g/4½ oz butter, diced

1 tbsp water

FILLING

150 ml/5 fl oz double cream

100 g/3½ oz caster sugar

4 eggs

grated rind of 3 lemons

175 ml/6 fl oz lemon juice

icing sugar, for dusting

COOK'S TIP

To avoid any spillage, pour half of the filling into the pastry case, place in the oven and pour in the remaining filling.

1 To make the pastry, place the flour and sugar in a bowl and rub in the butter with your fingertips until the mixture resembles breadcrumbs. Add the water. Bring together to form a dough. Wrap in clingfilm and chill in the refrigerator for 30 minutes.

2 Roll out the dough on a lightly floured work surface and line a 24-cm/9½-inch loose-bottomed quiche or flan tin. Prick the base of the pastry with a fork and chill in the refrigerator for 30 minutes.

3 Line the pastry case with foil and baking beans and bake in a preheated oven, 190°C/375°F/Gas Mark 5, for 15 minutes. Remove the foil and baking beans and cook the pastry case for a further 15 minutes.

4 To make the filling, whisk the cream, sugar, eggs, lemon rind and juice together until thoroughly blended. Place the pastry case, still in its tin, on a baking tray and pour in the filling (see Cook's Tip).

5 Bake the tart in the preheated oven for about 20 minutes, or until the filling is just set. Leave to cool, then remove the tart from the tin, dust with icing sugar and serve.

pine kernel tart

serves eight

PASTRY

150 g /5½ oz plain flour, plus extra
for dusting

25 g/1 oz caster sugar

125 g/4½ oz butter, diced

1 tbsp water

FILLING

350 g/12 oz curd cheese

4 tbsp double cream

3 eggs

125 g/4½ oz caster sugar

grated rind of 1 orange

100 g/3½ oz pine kernels

icing sugar, for dusting

1 To make the pastry, place the flour and sugar in a bowl and rub in the butter with your fingertips until the mixture resembles breadcrumbs. Add the water and bring together with your fingers to form a soft dough. Wrap in clingfilm and chill in the refrigerator for 30 minutes.

2 Roll out the dough on a lightly floured surface and line a 24-cm/9½-inch loose-bottomed quiche or flan tin. Prick the base of the pastry with a fork and leave to chill in the refrigerator for 30 minutes.

3 Line the pastry case with foil and baking beans and bake in a preheated oven, 190°C/375°F/Gas Mark 5, for 15 minutes. Remove the foil and baking beans and cook the pastry case for a further 15 minutes.

4 To make the filling, beat the curd cheese, cream, eggs, sugar, orange rind and half of the pine kernels together in a bowl. Pour the filling into the pastry case and sprinkle over the remaining pine kernels.

5 Reduce the oven temperature to 160°C/325°F/Gas Mark 3 and bake the tart for 35 minutes, or until just set. Leave to cool before removing from the tin, then dust with icing sugar and serve.

VARIATION

Replace the pine kernels with flaked almonds, if you prefer.

orange tart

PASTRY

150 g/5½ oz plain flour, plus extra
    for dusting

25 g/1 oz caster sugar

125 g /4½ oz butter, diced

1 tbsp water

FILLING

grated rind of 2 oranges

135 ml/4½ fl oz orange juice

50 g/1¾ oz fresh
    white breadcrumbs

2 tbsp lemon juice

150 ml/5 fl oz single cream

4 tbsp butter

50 g/1¾ oz caster sugar

2 eggs, separated

salt

TO SERVE

whipped cream

grated orange rind

1 To make the pastry, place the flour and sugar in a bowl and rub in the butter with your fingertips until the mixture resembles breadcrumbs. Add the water and bring the mixture together with your fingers to form a soft dough. Wrap in clingfilm and chill in the refrigerator for 30 minutes.

2 Roll out the dough on a lightly floured work surface and use it to line a 24-cm/9½-inch loose-bottomed quiche or flan tin. Prick the base of the pastry with a fork and leave to chill in the refrigerator for 30 minutes.

3 Line the pastry case with foil and baking beans and bake in a preheated oven, 190°C/375°F/Gas Mark 5, for 15 minutes. Remove the foil and baking beans and cook for a further 15 minutes.

4 To make the filling, mix the orange rind and juice and the breadcrumbs together in a bowl. Stir in the lemon juice and cream. Melt the butter and sugar in a saucepan over a low heat. Remove the saucepan from the heat, add the egg yolks, a pinch of salt and the breadcrumb mixture and stir.

5 Whisk the egg whites with a pinch of salt in a mixing bowl until they form soft peaks. Fold them into the egg yolk mixture.

6 Pour the filling into the pastry. Bake the tart in a preheated oven, 160°C/325°F/Gas Mark 3 for about 45 minutes, until set. Serve warm with whipped cream and orange rind.

coconut cream tart

PASTRY

150 g/5½ oz plain flour, plus extra
    for dusting

25 g/1 oz caster sugar

125 g/4½ oz butter, diced

1 tbsp water

FILLING

425 ml/15 fl oz milk

125 g/4½ oz creamed coconut

3 egg yolks

125 g/4½ oz caster sugar

50 g/1¾ oz plain flour, sieved

25 g/1 oz desiccated coconut, plus
    extra to decorate

25 g/1 oz glacé pineapple,
    chopped, plus extra to decorate

2 tbsp rum or pineapple juice

300 ml/10 fl oz whipping
    cream, whipped

1 To make the pastry, place the flour and sugar in a bowl and rub in the butter with your fingertips until the mixture resembles breadcrumbs. Add the water and bring the mixture together with your fingers to form a soft dough. Wrap in clingfilm and chill in the refrigerator for 30 minutes.

2 Roll out the dough on a lightly floured work surface and line a 24-cm/9½-inch loose-bottomed quiche or flan tin. Prick the base of the pastry with a fork and leave to chill in the refrigerator for 30 minutes.

3 Line the pastry case with foil and baking beans and bake in a preheated oven, 190°C/375°F/Gas Mark 5, for 15 minutes. Remove the foil and baking beans and cook the pastry case for a further 15 minutes. Leave to cool.

4 To make the filling, pour the milk into a small saucepan and add the creamed coconut. Set over a low heat and bring to just below boiling point, stirring, until the coconut has melted, then remove from the heat.

5 Whisk the egg yolks and sugar together in a bowl until pale and fluffy. Whisk in the flour. Pour the hot milk mixture over the egg mixture, stirring. Return the mixture to the saucepan and heat gently, stirring constantly, for 8 minutes, until thick. Leave to cool.

6 Stir in the coconut, pineapple and rum or juice. Spread in the pastry case, cover with cream, top with glacé pineapple and coconut, chill and serve.

apricot & cranberry tart

serves eight

PASTRY

150 g/5½ oz plain flour, plus extra
    for dusting

25 g/1 oz caster sugar

125 g/4½ oz butter, diced

1 tbsp water

FILLING

200 g/7 oz unsalted butter

200g/7 oz caster sugar

1 egg

2 egg yolks

5 tbsp plain flour, sieved

175 g/6 oz ground almonds

4 tbsp double cream

410 g/14½ oz canned apricot
    halves, drained

125 g/4½ oz fresh cranberries

1 To make the pastry, place the flour and sugar in a bowl and rub in the butter with your fingertips until the mixture resembles breadcrumbs. Add the water and bring the mixture together with your fingers to form a soft dough. Wrap in clingfilm and chill in the refrigerator for 30 minutes.

2 Roll out the dough on a lightly floured work surface and use it to line a 24-cm/9½-inch loose-bottomed quiche or flan tin. Prick the base of the pastry case all over with a fork and leave to chill in the refrigerator for 30 minutes.

3 Line the pastry case with foil and baking beans and bake in a preheated oven, 190°C/375°F/Gas

Mark 5 for 15 minutes. Remove the foil and baking beans and cook the pastry case for a further 10 minutes.

4 To make the filling, cream the butter and sugar together in a bowl until light and fluffy. Beat in the egg and egg yolks, then stir in the flour, almonds and cream.

5 Arrange the apricot halves and cranberries over the bottom of the pastry case and spoon the filling mixture over the top.

6 Bake in the preheated oven for about 1 hour, or until the topping is just set. Leave to cool slightly, then serve warm or cold.

cheese & apple tart

serves eight

1 tbsp butter, for greasing

175 g/6 oz self-raising flour

1 tsp baking powder

pinch of salt

75 g/2¾ oz soft brown sugar

100 g/3½ oz stoned dates, chopped

500 g/1lb 2 oz eating apples, cored
and chopped

50g /1¾ oz walnuts, chopped

50 ml/2 fl oz sunflower oil

2 eggs

175 g/6 oz grated Red
Leicester cheese

COOK'S TIP

This is a deliciously moist tart.
Any leftovers should be stored
in the refrigerator and heated
through before serving.

1 Grease a 23-cm/9½-inch loose-bottomed quiche or flan tin with the butter and line with baking paper.

2 Sieve the flour, baking powder and salt into a bowl. Stir in the brown sugar and the chopped dates, apples and walnuts. Mix together until well blended.

3 In a separate bowl, beat the oil and eggs together, then add the mixture to the dry ingredients. Stir until well blended.

4 Spoon half of the mixture into the prepared tin and level the surface with the back of a spoon.

5 Sprinkle with the grated cheese, then spoon over the remaining cake mixture, spreading it evenly to the edges of the tin.

6 Bake in a preheated oven, 180°C/350°F/Gas Mark 4, for 45–50 minutes, or until golden and firm to the touch.

7 Leave to cool slightly in the tin, then turn out and serve warm.

mincemeat & grape jalousie

1 tbsp butter, for greasing

plain flour, for dusting

500 g/1lb 2 oz fresh ready-made
    puff pastry, thawed if frozen

410 g/14½ oz mincemeat

100 g/3½ oz grapes, deseeded
    and halved

1 egg, lightly beaten, for glazing

demerara sugar, for sprinkling

COOK'S TIP

Puff pastry has a high proportion
of fat – this is what gives it its
characteristic layered appearance
and light, crisp texture. However,
this also makes it more fragile
than other types of pastry, so
handle it as lightly and as
little as possible.

VARIATION

For an enhanced festive flavour,
stir 2 tablespoons of sherry into
the mincemeat.

1 Lightly grease a baking tray with
the butter.

2 Roll out the pastry on a lightly
floured work surface, and cut it
into 2 rectangles.

3 Place 1 pastry rectangle on the
prepared baking tray and brush
the edges with a little water.

4 Mix the mincemeat and grapes
together in a mixing bowl. Spread
the mixture over the pastry rectangle
on the baking tray, leaving a 2.5-cm/
1-inch border.

5 Fold the second pastry rectangle
in half lengthways and carefully
cut a series of parallel lines across the
folded edge with a sharp knife, leaving
a 2.5-cm/1-inch border.

6 Open out the pastry rectangle and
lay it over the mincemeat, then
press the edges of the pastry firmly
together to seal.

7 Flute and crimp the edges of the
pastry with your fingertips. Lightly
brush with the beaten egg and sprinkle
with a little demerara sugar.

8 Bake the jalousie in a preheated
oven, 220°C/425°F/Gas Mark 7,
for 15 minutes. Reduce the heat to
180°C/350°F/Gas Mark 4 and cook for
a further 30 minutes, until the jalousie
is well risen and golden brown.

9 Transfer the jalousie to a wire rack
to cool completely before serving.

lime frangipane tartlets

makes twelve

125 g/4½ oz plain flour, plus extra
for dusting

100 g/3½ oz butter, softened

1 tsp grated lime rind

1 tbsp lime juice

50 g/1¾ oz caster sugar

1 egg

25 g/1 oz ground almonds

50 g/1¾ oz icing sugar, sieved

½ tbsp water

1 Reserve 5 teaspoons of the flour and 3 teaspoons of the butter and set aside until required.

2 Rub the remaining butter into the remaining flour with your fingertips until the mixture resembles fine breadcrumbs. Stir in the lime rind, followed by the lime juice, then bring the mixture together with your fingers to form a soft dough.

3 Roll out the dough thinly on a lightly floured surface. Stamp out 12 rounds, 7.5-cm/3-inches wide, with a fluted cutter, and line a bun tin.

4 Cream the reserved butter and the caster sugar together in a mixing bowl.

5 Mix in the egg, then the ground almonds and the reserved flour.

6 Divide the almond mixture between the pastry cases.

7 Bake in a preheated oven, 200°C/400°F/Gas Mark 6, for 15 minutes, until set and lightly golden. Turn the tartlets out on to a wire rack to cool.

8 Mix the icing sugar with the water. Drizzle a little of the icing over each tartlet and serve.

pear tarts

COOK'S TIP

If you prefer, serve these tarts
with vanilla ice cream for a
delicious dessert.

1 Roll out the pastry on a lightly floured work surface. Stamp out 6 x 10-cm/4-inch circles with a cutter.

2 Place the circles on a large baking tray and chill in the refrigerator for 30 minutes.

3 Cream the sugar and butter together in a small bowl, then stir in the chopped stem ginger.

4 Prick the pastry circles with a fork then spread with ginger mixture.

5 Slice the pear halves lengthways several times, keeping them intact at the tip. Fan out the slices slightly.

6 Place a pear half on top of each pastry circle. Make small flutes around the edges of the circles, then brush the pears with melted butter.

7 Bake in a preheated oven, 200°C/400°F/Gas Mark 6, for 15–20 minutes, until the pastry is risen and golden. Leave to cool slightly, then serve warm with a little cream.

crème brûlée tarts

serves six

PASTRY

150 g/5½ oz plain flour, plus extra
   for dusting

25 g/1 oz caster sugar

125 g/4½ oz butter, diced

1 tbsp water

FILLING

4 egg yolks

50 g/1¾ oz caster sugar

400 ml/14 fl oz double cream

1 tsp vanilla essence

demerara sugar, for sprinkling

1 To make the pastry, place the flour and sugar in a bowl and rub in the butter with your fingertips until the mixture resembles breadcrumbs. Add the water and bring the mixture together with your fingers to form a soft dough. Wrap in clingfilm and chill for 30 minutes.

2 Divide the dough into 6 pieces. Roll out each piece on a lightly floured work surface and use it to line 6 tartlet tins, 10 cm/4 inches wide. Prick the shells with a fork and chill in the refrigerator for 20 minutes.

3 Line the pastry cases with foil and baking beans and bake in a preheated oven, 190°C/375°F/ Gas Mark 5, for 15 minutes. Remove the foil and beans and cook the pastry cases for a further 10 minutes, until crisp. Leave to cool.

4 Meanwhile, make the filling. Beat the egg yolks and sugar together in a bowl until pale. Heat the cream and vanilla essence in a saucepan until just below boiling point, then pour it on to the egg mixture, whisking constantly.

5 Return the mixture to a clean saucepan and bring to just below the boil, stirring, until thick. Do not allow it to boil or it will curdle.

6 Leave to cool slightly, then pour into the tart cases. Leave to cool, then chill in the refrigerator overnight.

7 Sprinkle the tarts with sugar. Place under a preheated hot grill for a few minutes. Leave to cool, then chill for 2 hours before serving.

pavlova

serves six

3 egg whites

pinch of salt

175 g/6 oz caster sugar

300 ml/10 fl oz double cream,
   whipped lightly

fresh fruit of your choice (such as
   raspberries, strawberries,
   peaches or cape gooseberries)

1 Line a large baking tray with a sheet of baking paper, then whisk the egg whites with the salt in a large bowl until they form soft peaks.

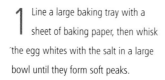

2 Whisk in the caster sugar, a little at a time, whisking well after each addition until all of the sugar has been incorporated.

3 Spoon three-quarters of the meringue onto the baking tray, forming a 20-cm/8-inch circle.

4 Place spoonfuls of the remaining meringue all around the edge of the round so they join up to make a rim, creating a nest shape.

5 Bake the meringue in a preheated oven, 140°C/275°F/Gas Mark 1, for 1¼ hours.

6 Turn the heat off, but leave the pavlova in the oven until it is completely cold.

7 Place the pavlova on a serving dish. Spread with the lightly whipped cream, then arrange the fresh fruit on top. Do not add the cream and fruit too far in advance or the pavlova will go soggy.

almond cheesecakes

serves four

12 amaretti biscuits

1 egg white, lightly beaten

225 g/8 oz skimmed-milk
   soft cheese

½ tsp almond essence

½ tsp finely grated lime rind

25 g/1 oz ground almonds

25 g/1 oz caster sugar

55 g/2 oz sultanas

2 tsp powdered gelatine

2 tbsp boiling water

2 tbsp lime juice

TO DECORATE

25 g/1 oz toasted flaked almonds

strips of lime rind

1 Place the biscuits in a clean plastic bag, seal the bag and, using a rolling pin, crush them into small pieces.

2 Place the crumbs in a bowl and bind together with the egg white.

3 Line a baking tray with baking paper or use a non-stick tray. Arrange 4 non-stick pastry rings or poached egg rings, 9 cm/3½ inches wide, on top, Divide the biscuit mixture into 4 equal portions and spoon it into the rings, pressing down well. Bake in a preheated oven, 180°C/350°F/Gas Mark 4, for 10 minutes, until crisp. Remove from the oven and leave to cool in the rings.

4 Beat the soft cheese in a bowl, then beat in the almond essence, lime rind, ground almonds, sugar and sultanas until thoroughly blended.

5 Dissolve the gelatine in the boiling water and stir in the lime juice. Fold into the cheese mixture and spoon over the biscuit bases. Smooth over the tops and chill in the refrigerator for 1 hour, or until set.

6 Loosen the cheesecakes from the tins using a small palette knife or spatula and transfer to serving plates. Decorate with toasted flaked almonds and strips of lime rind and serve.

baked bananas

serves four

4 bananas

2 passion fruit

4 tbsp orange juice

4 tbsp orange-flavoured liqueur

ORANGE-FLAVOURED CREAM

150 ml/5 fl oz double cream

3 tbsp icing sugar

2 tbsp orange-flavoured liqueur

VARIATION

Leave the bananas in their skins for a really quick dessert. Split the banana skins and pop in 1–2 squares of chocolate. Wrap the bananas in foil and bake for 10 minutes, or until the chocolate just melts.

1 To make the orange-flavoured cream, pour the double cream into a mixing bowl and sprinkle over the icing sugar. Whisk the mixture until it is standing in soft peaks. Carefully fold in the orange-flavoured liqueur and chill the cream in the refrigerator until required.

2 Peel the bananas and place each one on to a sheet of foil.

3 Cut the passion fruit in half and squeeze the juice of each half over each banana. Spoon orange juice and liqueur over each banana.

4 Fold the foil sheets over the top of the bananas so they are completely enclosed.

5 Place the parcels on a baking tray and bake the bananas in a preheated oven, 180°C/350°F/Gas Mark 4, for about 10 minutes, or until they are just tender (test by inserting a cocktail stick).

6 Transfer the foil parcels to warmed serving plates. Open out the parcels at the table, then serve immediately with the chilled orange-flavoured cream.

baked apples with berries

serves four

4 medium cooking apples

1 tbsp lemon juice

100 g/3½ oz prepared blackberries,
thawed if frozen

15 g/½ oz flaked almonds

½ tsp ground mixed spice

½ tsp finely grated lemon rind

2 tbsp demerara sugar

300 ml/10 fl oz ruby port

1 cinnamon stick, broken

2 tsp cornflour blended with 2 tbsp
cold water

low-fat custard, to serve

1 Wash and dry the apples. Make a shallow cut through the skin around the middle of each apple using a small sharp knife – this will help the apples to cook through.

2 Core the apples, brush the centres with the lemon juice to prevent them from discolouring, then stand them in an ovenproof dish.

3 Mix the berries, almonds, mixed spice, lemon rind and sugar in a bowl. Spoon the mixture into the centre of each apple using a teaspoon.

4 Pour the port into the dish, add the cinnamon stick and bake the apples in a preheated oven, 200°C/ 400°F/Gas Mark 6, for 35–40 minutes, or until tender and soft.

5 Drain the cooking juices into a saucepan and keep the apples warm in the oven on a very low heat.

6 Remove the cinnamon, then add the cornflour mixture to the cooking juices. Cook over a medium heat, stirring constantly, until thickened.

7 Heat the low-fat custard until piping hot. Pour the sauce over the apples and serve with the custard.

baked pears with cinnamon

serves four

4 ripe pears

2 tbsp lemon juice

4 tbsp light muscovado sugar

1 tsp ground cinnamon

55 g/2 oz low-fat spread

finely shredded lemon rind,
    to decorate

low-fat custard, to serve

1 Core and peel the pears, then slice them in half lengthways and brush them all over with the lemon juice to prevent them from discolouring. Place the pear halves, cored sides down, in a small non-stick roasting tin.

2 Place the sugar, cinnamon and low-fat spread in a small saucepan over a low heat, stirring constantly, until the sugar has dissolved. Keep the heat very low to stop too much water evaporating from the low-fat spread as it starts to get hot. Spoon the mixture over the pears.

3 Bake the pears in a preheated oven, 200°C/400°F/Gas Mark 6, for 20–25 minutes, or until they are tender and golden, occasionally spooning the sugar mixture over the fruit during the cooking time.

4 To serve, heat the low-fat custard until it is piping hot and spoon a little over the base of each of 4 warmed dessert plates, then arrange 2 pear halves on each plate.

5 Decorate the pears with a little finely shredded lemon rind and serve immediately.

italian bread pudding

serves four

1 tbsp butter, for greasing

2 small eating apples, peeled, cored
and sliced into rings

75 g/2¾ oz granulated sugar

2 tbsp white wine

100 g/3½ oz bread, sliced, with
crusts removed (a slightly stale
French bread stick is ideal)

300 ml/10 fl oz single cream

2 eggs, beaten

pared rind of 1 orange, cut
into matchsticks

VARIATION

For a change, try adding some
dried fruit, such as apricots,
cherries or dates, to the pudding,
if you wish.

---

1 Grease a 1.2-litre/2-pint deep
ovenproof dish with the butter.

2 Arrange the apple rings across the
base of the dish, overlapping
them, then sprinkle half of the sugar
over the apples.

3 Pour the wine over the apples.
Add the bread slices, pushing
them down with your hands to flatten
them slightly.

4 Mix the cream with the eggs, the
remaining sugar and the orange
rind and pour the mixture over the
bread. Leave to soak for 30 minutes.

5 Bake the pudding in a preheated
oven, 180°C/350°F/Gas Mark 4,
for 25 minutes, until golden and set.
Remove from the oven, leave to cool
slightly and serve warm.

COOK'S TIP

Some varieties of eating apples
are better for cooking than
others. Among the most suitable
are Blenheim Orange, Cox's
Orange Pippin, Egremont Russet,
Granny Smith, Idared, James
Grieve, Jonagold, Jonathan.
McIntosh, Northern Spy
and Winesap.

tuscan pudding

serves four

1 tbsp butter, for greasing

75 g/2¾ oz mixed dried fruit

250 g/9 oz ricotta cheese

3 egg yolks

50 g/1¾ oz caster sugar

1 tsp ground cinnamon

finely grated rind of 1 orange, plus

    extra to decorate

crème fraîche, to serve (optional)

COOK'S TIP

Crème fraîche has a slightly sour, nutty taste and is very thick. It is suitable for cooking, but has the same fat content as double cream. It can be made by stirring cultured buttermilk into double cream and chilling in the refrigerator overnight.

1 Lightly grease 4 mini pudding basins or ramekin dishes with the butter.

2 Place the dried fruit in a bowl and cover with warm water. Leave to soak for 10 minutes.

3 Beat the ricotta cheese with the egg yolks in a bowl. Stir in the caster sugar, cinnamon and orange rind and mix well.

4 Drain the dried fruit in a sieve set over a bowl. Mix the drained fruit with the ricotta cheese mixture.

5 Spoon the mixture into the prepared basins or dishes.

6 Bake in a preheated oven, 180°C/ 350°F/Gas Mark 4, for 15 minutes. The tops should be firm to the touch but should not have browned.

7 Decorate the puddings with grated orange rind. Serve warm or chilled with a spoonful of crème fraîche, if you wish.

mascarpone cheesecake

serves eight

1½ tbsp unsalted butter, plus extra
    for greasing
150 g/5½ oz ginger biscuits, crushed
25 g/1 oz stem ginger, chopped
500 g/1 lb 2 oz mascarpone cheese
finely grated rind and juice of
    2 lemons
100 g/3½ oz caster sugar
2 large eggs, separated
fruit coulis (see Cook's Tip), to serve

COOK'S TIP

Fruit coulis can be made
by cooking 400 g/14 oz of
fruit, such as blueberries, for
5 minutes with 2 tablespoons of
water. Sieve the mixture, then stir
in 1 tablespoon (or more to taste)
of sifted icing sugar. Leave to
cool before serving.

1 Grease the base of a 25-cm/
10-inch springform cake tin or
loose-bottomed tin with butter and
line with baking paper.

2 Melt the butter in a saucepan
over a low heat and stir in the
crushed biscuits and stem ginger. Use
the mixture to line the tin, pressing it
about 5 mm/¼ inch up the sides.

3 Beat the cheese, lemon rind and
juice, sugar and egg yolks
together in a bowl until quite smooth.

4 Whisk the egg whites until stiff.
Fold into the cheese mixture.

5 Pour the mixture over the biscuit
base in the prepared tin and bake
in a preheated oven, 180°C/350°F/
Gas Mark 4, for 35–45 minutes, until
just set. Don't worry if it cracks or sinks
– this is quite normal.

6 Leave the cheesecake in the tin
to cool. Serve with fruit coulis
(see Cook's Tip).

honey & nut nests

serves four

225 g/8 oz angel hair pasta

115 g/4 oz butter

175 g/6 oz shelled pistachio
nuts, chopped

115 g/4 oz sugar

115 g/4 oz clear honey

150 ml/5 fl oz water

2 tsp lemon juice

salt

Greek-style yogurt, to serve

COOK'S TIP

Angel hair pasta is also
known as capelli d'angelo. It is
long and very fine, and is usually
sold in small bunches that
resemble nests.

1 Bring a large saucepan of lightly
salted water to the boil. Add the
pasta and cook for 8–10 minutes, or
until tender but still firm to the bite.
Drain the pasta and return to the pan.
Add the butter and toss to coat the
pasta thoroughly. Leave the pasta to
cool completely.

2 Arrange 4 small flan or poaching
rings on a baking tray. Divide the
angel hair pasta into 8 equal portions
and spoon 1 portion into each ring.
Press down lightly. Top the pasta
with half of the nuts, then add the
remaining pasta portions.

3 Bake in a preheated oven,
180°C/350°F/Gas Mark 4 for
45 minutes, or until golden brown.

4 Meanwhile, put the sugar,
honey and water into a saucepan
and bring to the boil over a low heat,
stirring constantly, until the sugar has
dissolved completely. Simmer for
10 minutes, add the lemon juice and
simmer for 5 minutes.

5 Carefully transfer the angel hair
nests to a serving dish using a
spatula or fish slice. Pour over the
honey syrup, sprinkle over the
remaining nuts and leave to cool
completely before serving. Hand the
Greek-style yogurt separately.

banana pastries

serves four

PASTRY

450 g/1 lb plain flour, plus extra
   for dusting

4 tbsp lard

4 tbsp unsalted butter

125 ml/4 fl oz water

FILLING

2 large bananas

75 g/2¾ oz finely chopped no-soak
   dried apricots

pinch of nutmeg

dash of orange juice

1 egg yolk, beaten

icing sugar, for dusting

1 To make the pastry, sift the flour into a large mixing bowl. Add the lard and butter and rub into the flour with your fingertips until the mixture resembles breadcrumbs. Gradually blend in the water and bring together with your fingers to form a soft dough. Wrap in clingfilm and chill in the refrigerator for 30 minutes.

2 To make the filling, mash the bananas in a bowl with a fork and stir in the apricots, nutmeg and orange juice, mixing well.

3 Roll the dough out on a lightly floured surface and stamp out 16 rounds, 10 cm/4 inches wide.

4 Spoon a little banana filling on to one half of each round and fold the dough over the filling to make semi-circles. Pinch the edges together and seal by pressing with a fork.

5 Arrange the pastries on a non-stick baking tray and brush them with the beaten egg yolk. Cut a small slit in each pastry and cook in a preheated oven, 180°C/350°F/Gas Mark 4, for about 25 minutes, or until golden brown and crisp.

6 Dust the banana pastries with icing sugar and serve.

chinese custard tarts

makes fifteen

PASTRY

175 g/6 oz plain flour, plus extra
  for dusting

3 tbsp caster sugar

4 tbsp unsalted butter

2 tbsp lard

2 tbsp water

CUSTARD

2 small eggs

55 g/2 oz caster sugar

175 ml/6 fl oz milk

½ tsp ground nutmeg, plus extra
  for sprinkling

cream, to serve

1 To make the pastry, sift the flour into a bowl. Add the sugar and rub in the butter and lard with your fingertips until the mixture resembles breadcrumbs. Add the water and bring together with your fingertips to form a firm dough.

2 Transfer the dough to a lightly floured surface and knead for about 5 minutes, until smooth. Form into a ball, cover with clingfilm and chill in the refrigerator while you prepare the filling.

3 To make the custard, beat the eggs and sugar together. Gradually add the milk and ground nutmeg and beat until well blended.

4 Separate the dough into 15 even-sized pieces. Flatten the dough pieces into rounds and press into shallow tartlet tins.

5 Spoon the custard into the pastry cases and cook in a preheated oven, 150°C/300°F/Gas Mark 2, for 25–30 minutes.

6 Transfer the Chinese custard tarts to a wire rack, leave to cool slightly, then sprinkle with extra ground nutmeg. Serve warm or cold with cream.

Cakes & Bread

There is nothing more traditional than afternoon tea and cakes and this chapter gives a wickedly extravagant twist to some of those delicious tea-time classics – full of chocolate, spice and all things nice, these recipes are a treat to enjoy. The chapter includes a variety of different cakes depending on the time you have and the effort you want to spend. Small cakes include Cranberry Muffins, Almond Slices, and Treacle Scones. These cakes are easier to prepare and cook than larger ones and, in general, are particular favourites with children and adults alike.

cinnamon & currant loaf

makes one loaf

150 g/5½ oz butter, diced, plus
    extra for greasing
350 g/12 oz plain flour
pinch of salt
1 tbsp baking powder
1 tbsp ground cinnamon
125 g/4½ oz soft brown sugar
175 g/6 oz currants
finely grated rind of 1 orange
5–6 tbsp orange juice
6 tbsp milk
2 eggs, beaten lightly

1 Grease a 900-g/2-lb loaf tin with a little butter and line the base with baking paper.

2 Sieve the flour, salt, baking powder and cinnamon into a bowl. Rub in the butter with your fingertips until the mixture resembles coarse breadcrumbs.

3 Stir in the sugar, currants and orange rind. Beat the orange juice, milk and eggs together and add to the dry ingredients. Mix well.

4 Spoon the mixture into the prepared tin. Make a slight dip in the centre to help the loaf rise evenly.

5 Bake in a preheated oven, 180°C/350°F/Gas Mark 4, for about 1–1 hour 10 minutes, or until a fine metal skewer inserted into the centre of the loaf comes out clean.

6 Leave the loaf to cool before turning out of the tin. Transfer to a wire rack and leave to cool completely before slicing and serving.

COOK'S TIP
Once you have added the liquid to the dry ingredients, work as quickly as possible, because the baking powder is activated by the liquid.

banana & cranberry loaf

makes one loaf

1 tbsp butter, for greasing

175 g/6 oz self-raising flour

½ tsp baking powder

150 g/5½ oz soft brown sugar

2 bananas, mashed

50 g/1¾ oz chopped mixed peel

25 g/1 oz chopped mixed nuts

50 g/1¾ oz dried cranberries

5–6 tbsp orange juice

2 eggs, lightly beaten

150 ml/5 fl oz sunflower oil

75 g/2¾ oz icing sugar, sieved

grated rind of 1 orange

COOK'S TIP

This tea bread will keep for a couple of days. Wrap it carefully and store in a cool, dry place.

1 Grease a 900-g/2-lb loaf tin with the butter and line the base with baking paper.

2 Sieve the flour and baking powder into a mixing bowl. Stir in the sugar, bananas, chopped mixed peel, nuts and dried cranberries.

3 In a separate bowl, mix the orange juice, eggs and oil until well blended. Add the mixture to the dry ingredients and mix well. Spoon the mixture into the prepared tin and level the surface with a palette knife.

4 Bake in a preheated oven, 180°C/350°F/Gas Mark 4, for about 1 hour, until firm to the touch or until a fine metal skewer inserted into the centre of the loaf comes out clean.

5 Turn out the loaf on to a wire rack and leave to cool.

6 Mix the icing sugar with a little water and drizzle the icing over the loaf. Sprinkle orange rind over the top. Leave the icing to set before serving the loaf in slices.

banana & date loaf

makes one loaf

100 g/3½ oz butter, diced, plus
    extra for greasing
225 g/8 oz self-raising flour
75 g/2¾ oz caster sugar
125 g/4½ oz stoned dried
    dates, chopped
2 bananas, mashed roughly
2 eggs, beaten lightly
2 tbsp clear honey

COOK'S TIP

This tea bread will keep for
several days if stored in an
airtight container and kept
in a cool, dry place.

VARIATION

Substitute other dried fruit, such
as prunes or apricots, for the
dates. Use no-soak varieties for
the best results.

1 Grease a 900-g/2-lb loaf tin with
a little butter and line the base
with baking paper.

2 Sieve the flour into a large mixing
bowl. Rub the butter into the flour
with your fingertips until the mixture
resembles fine breadcrumbs.

3 Stir the sugar, dates, bananas,
eggs and honey into the dry
ingredients and mix well.

4 Spoon the mixture into the
prepared loaf tin and level the
surface with a palette knife.

5 Bake in a preheated oven,
160°C/325°F/Gas Mark 3, for
about 1 hour, or until golden brown
and a fine metal skewer inserted into
the centre of the loaf comes out clean.

6 Leave the loaf to cool for
10 minutes before turning out
of the tin. Transfer to a wire rack and
leave to cool completely.

7 Serve the loaf warm or cold, cut
into thick slices.

fruit loaf with apple spread

makes one loaf

1 tbsp butter, for greasing

175 g/6 oz rolled oats

1 tsp ground cinnamon

100 g/3½ oz light muscovado sugar

125 g/4½ oz sultanas

175 g/6 oz seedless raisins

2 tbsp malt extract

300 ml/10 fl oz unsweetened
    apple juice

175 g/6 oz wholemeal
    self-raising flour

1½ tsp baking powder

FRUIT SPREAD

225 g/8 oz strawberries, washed
    and hulled

2 eating apples, cored, chopped
    and mixed with 1 tbsp
    lemon juice

300 ml/10 fl oz unsweetened
    apple juice

TO SERVE

strawberries

apple wedges

1 Grease a 900-g/2-lb loaf tin and line with baking paper. Place the oats, cinnamon, sugar, sultanas, raisins and malt extract in a bowl. Stir in the apple juice. Set aside for 30 minutes.

2 Sift in the flour and baking powder, adding any bran that remains in the sieve, and fold in using a metal spoon.

3 Spoon the mixture into the prepared tin and bake in a preheated oven, 180°C/350°F/Gas Mark 4, for 1½ hours, until firm or until a fine metal skewer inserted into the centre of the loaf comes out clean.

4 Leave the loaf to cool in the tin for 10 minutes. Turn out on to a wire rack and leave to cool completely.

5 Meanwhile, to make the fruit spread, place the strawberries and apples in a saucepan and pour in the apple juice. Bring to the boil over a low heat, cover and simmer gently for 30 minutes. Beat the sauce well and spoon into a sterilized, warmed jar. Leave to cool, then seal and label.

6 Serve the fruit loaf, cut into slices, with 1–2 tablespoons of the fruit spread and an assortment of strawberries and apple wedges.

cranberry muffins

makes eighteen

1 tbsp butter, for greasing

225 g/8 oz plain flour

2 tsp baking powder

½ tsp salt

50 g/1¾ oz caster sugar

4 tbsp butter, melted

2 eggs, beaten

200 ml/7 fl oz milk

100 g/3½ oz fresh cranberries

35 g/1¼ oz freshly grated
   Parmesan cheese

1 Lightly grease 2 bun tins with the butter. Sieve the flour, baking powder and salt into a mixing bowl. Stir in the caster sugar.

2 In a separate bowl, mix the butter, beaten eggs and milk together, then pour into the dry ingredients. Mix lightly together until all of the ingredients are evenly blended, then stir in the cranberries.

3 Divide the mixture between the prepared tins.

4 Sprinkle the grated Parmesan over the top of each portion of the muffin mixture.

5 Bake in a preheated oven, 200°C/ 400°F/Gas Mark 6, for about 20 minutes, or until the muffins are well risen and golden brown.

6 Leave the muffins to cool in the tins for 10 minutes, then transfer to a wire rack and leave to cool completely before serving.

date & honey loaf

makes one loaf

1 tbsp butter, for greasing

250 g/9 oz strong white bread flour,
    plus extra for dusting

75 g/2¾ oz strong brown
    bread flour

½ tsp salt

1 sachet easy-blend dried yeast

200 ml/7 fl oz hand-hot water

3 tbsp sunflower oil

3 tbsp clear honey

75 g/2¾ oz dried dates, stoned
    and chopped

2 tbsp sesame seeds

COOK'S TIP

If you cannot find a warm
place, sit a bowl with the dough
in it over a small saucepan of
warm water and cover.

1 Grease a 900-g/2-lb loaf tin with the butter.

2 Sieve the white and brown flours into a large mixing bowl and stir in the salt and dried yeast. Pour in the water, oil and honey. Bring together with your fingers to form a dough.

3 Place the dough on a lightly floured work surface and knead for about 5 minutes, until smooth.

4 Place the dough in a greased bowl, cover and leave to rise in a warm place for about 1 hour, or until doubled in size.

5 Knead in the dates and sesame seeds. Shape the dough and place in the tin.

6 Cover and leave in a warm place for a further 30 minutes, or until springy to the touch.

7 Bake in a preheated oven, 220°C/425°F/Gas Mark 7 for 30 minutes. When the loaf is cooked, it should sound hollow when tapped on the base.

8 Transfer the loaf to a wire rack and leave to cool completely. Serve cut into thick slices.

mango twist bread

makes one loaf

3 tbsp butter, diced, plus extra
    for greasing
450 g/1 lb strong white bread flour,
    plus extra for dusting
1 tsp salt
1 sachet easy-blend dried yeast
1 tsp ground ginger
50 g/1¾ oz soft brown sugar
1 small mango, peeled, stoned
    and puréed
250 ml/9 fl oz hand-hot water
2 tbsp clear honey
125 g/4½ oz sultanas
1 egg, beaten lightly
icing sugar, for dusting

1 Grease a baking tray with a little butter. Sieve the flour and salt into a large mixing bowl, stir in the yeast, ground ginger and brown sugar. Rub in the butter with your fingertips.

2 Stir in the mango purée, water and honey and bring together with your fingers to form a dough.

3 Place the dough on a lightly floured work surface. Knead for 5 minutes, until smooth. Alternatively, use an electric mixer with a dough hook. Place the dough in a greased bowl, cover and leave to rise in a warm place for about 1 hour, until it has doubled in size.

4 Knead in the sultanas and shape the dough into 2 sausage shapes, each 25 cm/10 inches long. Carefully twist the 2 pieces together and pinch the ends to seal. Place the dough on the baking tray, cover and leave in a warm place for a further 40 minutes.

5 Brush the loaf with the egg. Bake in a preheated oven, 220°C/425°F/Gas Mark 7, for 30 minutes, or until golden. Cool on a wire rack and dust with icing sugar before serving.

COOK'S TIP
You can tell when the bread is
cooked as it will sound hollow
when tapped on the bottom.

citrus bread

makes one loaf

4 tbsp butter, diced, plus extra
    for greasing

450 g/1 lb strong white bread flour,
    plus extra for dusting

½ tsp salt

50 g/1¾ oz caster sugar

1 sachet easy-blend dried yeast

5–6 tbsp orange juice

4 tbsp lemon juice

3–4 tbsp lime juice

150 ml/5 fl oz hand-hot water

1 orange

1 lemon

1 lime

2 tbsp clear honey, for glazing

1 Lightly grease a baking tray with a little butter.

2 Sieve the flour and salt into a large mixing bowl. Stir in the sugar and dried yeast.

3 Rub the butter into the mixture with your fingertips until the mixture resembles breadcrumbs. Add the orange juice, lemon juice, lime juice and water and bring together with your fingers to form a dough.

4 Place the dough on a lightly floured work surface and knead for 5 minutes. Alternatively, use an electric mixer with a dough hook. Place the dough in a greased bowl, cover and leave to rise in a warm place for about 1 hour, until doubled in size.

5 Meanwhile, grate the rind of the orange, lemon and lime. Knead the fruit rinds into the dough.

6 Divide the dough into 2 balls, making one slightly bigger than the other.

7 Place the larger ball on the baking tray and set the smaller one on top.

8 Push a floured finger through the centre of the dough. Cover and leave to rise for about 40 minutes, or until springy to the touch.

9 Bake in a preheated oven, 220°C/425°F/Gas Mark 7 for 35 minutes. Remove from the oven and transfer to a wire rack to cool. Glaze with the clear honey.

crown loaf

makes one loaf

2 tbsp butter, diced, plus extra
   for greasing

225 g/8 oz strong white bread flour

½ tsp salt

1 sachet easy-blend dried yeast

125 ml/4 fl oz hand-hot milk

1 egg, beaten lightly

FILLING

4 tbsp butter, softened

50 g/1¾ oz soft brown sugar

25 g/1 oz chopped hazelnuts

25 g/1 oz stem ginger, chopped

50 g/1¾ oz mixed peel

1 tbsp rum or brandy

ICING

100 g/3½ oz icing sugar

2 tbsp lemon juice

1 Grease a baking sheet with a little butter. Sieve the flour and salt into a large mixing bowl. Stir in the yeast. Rub in the butter with your fingertips. Add the milk and egg and bring together with your fingers to form a dough.

2 Place the dough in a greased bowl, cover and leave in a warm place for about 40 minutes, until doubled in size. Knead the dough lightly for 1 minute to knock it back. Roll out into a rectangle measuring 30 x 23 cm/12 x 9 inches.

3 To make the filling, cream the butter and sugar together in a large bowl until the mixture is light and fluffy. Stir in the hazelnuts, stem ginger, mixed peel and rum or brandy. Spread the filling over the dough, leaving a 2.5-cm/1-inch border all around.

4 Roll up the dough, starting from the long edge, to form a sausage shape. Cut the dough roll into slices at 5-cm/2-inch intervals and place on the baking tray in a circle with the slices just touching. Cover and leave to rise in a warm place for 30 minutes.

5 Bake in a preheated oven, 190°C/325°F/Gas Mark 5, for about 20–30 minutes, or until golden. Meanwhile, mix the icing sugar with enough lemon juice to form a thin, runny icing.

6 Leave the loaf to cool slightly on a wire rack before drizzling with icing. Allow the icing to set slightly before serving.

chocolate bread

makes one loaf

1 tbsp butter, for greasing

450 g/1 lb strong white bread flour,
   plus extra for dusting

25 g/1 oz cocoa powder

1 tsp salt

1 sachet easy-blend dried yeast

25 g/1 oz soft brown sugar

1 tbsp oil

300 ml/10 fl oz hand-hot water

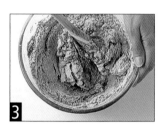

3 Pour in the oil with the water and mix the ingredients together to form a dough.

4 Place the dough on a lightly floured work surface and knead for 5 minutes. Alternatively, use an electric mixer with a dough hook.

5 Place the dough in a greased bowl, cover and leave to rise in a warm place for about 1 hour, or until it has doubled in size.

6 Knead the dough lightly for about 1 minute to knock it back, then shape it into a loaf. Place it in the prepared tin, cover and leave to rise in a warm place for a further 30 minutes.

7 Bake in a preheated oven, 200°C/400°F/Gas Mark 6, for 25–30 minutes. When the loaf is cooked it should sound hollow when tapped on the base.

1 Lightly grease a 900-g/2-lb loaf tin with the butter.

2 Sieve the flour and cocoa powder into a large mixing bowl. Stir in the salt, dried yeast and sugar.

8 Transfer the bread to a wire rack and leave to cool. Cut into slices and serve.

cinnamon swirls

makes twelve

2 tbsp butter, diced, plus extra
　for greasing
225 g/8 oz strong white bread flour,
　plus extra for dusting
½ tsp salt
1 sachet easy-blend dried yeast
1 egg, beaten
125 ml/4 fl oz hand-hot milk
2 tbsp maple syrup
FILLING
4 tbsp butter, softened
2 tsp ground cinnamon
50 g/1¾ oz soft brown sugar
50 g/1¾ oz currants

1 Grease a 23-cm/9-inch square
baking tin with a little butter.

2 Sieve the flour and salt into
a large mixing bowl. Stir in the
dried yeast. Rub in the butter with your
fingertips until the mixture resembles
fine breadcrumbs. Add the egg and
milk and bring together with your
fingers to form a dough.

3 Place the dough in a greased
bowl, cover and leave in a warm
place for about 40 minutes, or until
doubled in size.

4 Knead the dough lightly for about
1 minute to knock it back, then
roll out on a lightly floured surface
into a rectangle measuring 30 x 23 cm/
12 x 9 inches.

5 To make the filling, cream the
butter, cinnamon and brown
sugar together in a bowl until the
mixture is light and fluffy. Spread the
filling over the dough, leaving a
2.5-cm/1-inch border around the
edges. Sprinkle over the currants.

6 Roll up the dough like a Swiss
roll, starting at a long edge, and
press down to seal. Cut the roll into
12 slices. Place them in the tin, cover
and leave in a warm place for about
30 minutes.

7 Bake the slices in a preheated
oven, 190°C/375°F/Gas Mark 5,
for 20–30 minutes, or until well risen
and golden. Brush the swirls with the
maple syrup and leave to cool slightly.
Serve warm.

crunchy fruit cake

serves eight

100 g/3½ oz butter, softened, plus
   extra for greasing

100g/3½ oz caster sugar

2 eggs, beaten

50 g/1¾ oz self-raising flour, sieved

1 tsp baking powder

100 g/3½ oz polenta

225 g/8 oz mixed dried fruit

25 g/1 oz pine kernels

grated rind of 1 lemon

4 tbsp lemon juice

2 tbsp milk

VARIATION

To give a crumblier, light fruit
cake, omit the polenta and
use 150 g/5½ oz of self-raising
flour instead.

---

1 Grease an 18-cm/7-inch cake tin
with a little butter and line the
base with baking paper.

2 Whisk the butter and sugar
together in a bowl until light
and fluffy.

3 Whisk in the beaten eggs, a little
at a time, whisking thoroughly
after each addition.

4 Gently fold the flour, baking
powder and polenta into the
mixture until thoroughly blended.

5 Stir in the mixed dried fruit, pine
kernels, grated lemon rind, lemon
juice and milk.

6 Spoon the mixture into the
prepared tin and level the surface.

7 Bake in a preheated oven, 180°C/
350°F/Gas Mark 4, for about
1 hour, or until a fine metal skewer
inserted into the centre of the cake
comes out clean.

8 Leave the cake to cool in the tin
before turning out.

clementine cake

serves eight

175 g/6 oz butter, softened, plus
    extra for greasing

2 clementines

175 g/6 oz caster sugar

3 eggs, beaten

175 g/6 oz self-raising flour

3 tbsp ground almonds

3 tbsp single cream

GLAZE AND TOPPING

6 tbsp clementine juice

2 tbsp caster sugar

3 white sugar cubes, crushed

COOK'S TIP

If you prefer, chop the rind
from the clementines in a food
processor or blender together
with the sugar in step 2. Tip
the mixture into a bowl with
the butter and begin to
cream the mixture.

1 Grease an 18-cm/7-inch round
cake tin with a little butter and
line the base with baking paper.

2 Pare the rind from the clementines
and chop the rind finely. Cream
the butter, sugar and clementine rind
together in a bowl until pale and fluffy.

3 Gradually add the beaten eggs to
the mixture, beating thoroughly
after each addition.

4 Gently fold in the flour followed
by the ground almonds and the
single cream. Spoon the mixture into
the prepared tin.

5 Bake in a preheated oven,
180°C/350°F/Gas Mark 4, for
55–60 minutes, or until a fine metal
skewer inserted into the centre comes
out clean. Leave in the tin to cool for
10 minutes.

6 Meanwhile, to make the glaze,
put the clementine juice into a
small saucepan with the sugar. Bring
to the boil over a low heat and simmer
for 5 minutes.

7 Turn the cake out on to a wire
rack. Drizzle the glaze over the
cake until it has been absorbed and
sprinkle with the crushed sugar cubes.

caraway madeira

serves eight

225 g/8 oz butter, softened, plus
   extra for greasing

175 g/6 oz soft brown sugar

3 eggs, beaten

350 g/12 oz self-raising flour

1 tbsp caraway seeds

grated rind of 1 lemon

6 tbsp milk

1 or 2 strips of citron peel

1 Grease a 900-g/2-lb loaf tin with butter and line with baking paper.

2 Cream the butter and brown sugar together in a bowl until the mixture is pale and fluffy.

3 Gradually add the beaten eggs to the creamed mixture, beating thoroughly after each addition.

4 Sieve the flour into the bowl and gently fold into the creamed mixture in a figure-of-eight movement.

5 Add the caraway seeds, lemon rind and the milk and fold in until thoroughly blended.

6 Spoon the mixture into the prepared tin and level the surface.

7 Bake in a preheated oven, 160°C/325°F/Gas Mark 3, for 20 minutes.

8 Remove the cake from the oven, place the strips of citron peel on top and return to the oven for a further 40 minutes, or until the cake is well risen and a fine metal skewer inserted into the centre comes out clean.

9 Leave the cake to cool in the tin for 10 minutes before turning out and transferring to a wire rack to cool completely. Serve in slices when cold.

COOK'S TIP

Citron peel is available in the baking section of supermarkets. If it is unavailable, you can substitute chopped mixed peel.

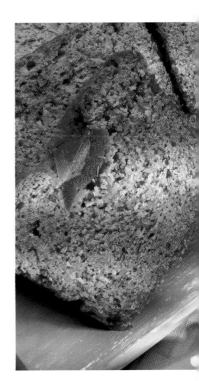

orange kugelhopf cake

serves four

225 g/8 oz butter, softened, plus
  extra for greasing
225 g/8 oz caster sugar
4 eggs, separated
425 g/15 oz plain flour, plus extra
  for dusting
pinch of salt
3 tsp baking powder
300 ml/10 fl oz fresh orange juice
1 tbsp orange flower water
1 tsp grated orange rind
SYRUP
200 ml/7 fl oz orange juice
200 g/7 oz granulated sugar

1 Grease and flour a 25-cm/10-inch kugelhopf tin or deep ring mould.

2 Cream the butter and caster sugar together in a bowl until the mixture is light and fluffy. Add the egg yolks, one at a time, whisking the mixture thoroughly after each addition.

3 Sieve the flour, salt and baking powder into a separate bowl. Gently fold the dry ingredients and the orange juice alternately into the creamed mixture with a metal spoon, working as lightly as possible, then stir in the orange flower water and the orange rind.

4 Whisk the egg whites until they form soft peaks, then fold them into the mixture in a figure-of-eight movement.

5 Pour the mixture into the prepared tin or mould and bake in a preheated oven, 180°C/350°F/ Gas Mark 4, for about 50–55 minutes, or until a metal skewer inserted into the centre of the cake comes out clean.

6 To make the syrup, put the orange juice and sugar in a saucepan and bring to the boil over a low heat. Simmer for 5 minutes, until the sugar has dissolved.

7 Remove the cake from the oven and leave to cool in the tin for 10 minutes. Prick the top of the cake with a fine metal skewer and brush over half of the syrup. Leave the cake to cool for another 10 minutes. Invert the cake on to a wire rack placed over a deep plate and brush the syrup over the cake until it is completely covered. Serve warm or cold.

lemon syrup cake

serves eight

1 tbsp butter, for greasing

200 g/7 oz plain flour

2 tsp baking powder

200 g/7 oz caster sugar

4 eggs

150 ml/5 fl oz soured cream

grated rind of 1 large lemon

4 tbsp lemon juice

150 ml/5 fl oz sunflower oil

SYRUP

4 tbsp icing sugar

3 tbsp lemon juice

1 Lightly grease a 20-cm/8-inch loose-bottomed round cake tin with the butter and line the base with baking paper.

2 Sieve the flour and baking powder into a large mixing bowl and stir in the caster sugar.

3 In a separate bowl or jug, whisk the eggs, soured cream, lemon rind, lemon juice and oil together.

4 Pour the egg mixture into the dry ingredients and mix thoroughly until evenly blended.

5 Pour the mixture into the prepared tin and bake in a preheated oven, 180°C/350°F/Gas Mark 4, for about 45–60 minutes, until well risen and golden brown on top.

6 To make the syrup, mix the icing sugar and lemon juice together in a small saucepan. Stir over a low heat until bubbling and just turning syrupy.

7 As soon as the cake comes out of the oven, prick the surface with a metal skewer, then brush syrup over the top. Leave to cool completely in the tin before turning out and serving.

COOK'S TIP

Pricking the surface of the hot cake with a skewer ensures that the syrup seeps into the cake and the full flavour is absorbed.

apple cake with cider

serves eight

6 tbsp butter, diced, plus extra
    for greasing

225 g/8 oz self-raising flour

1 tsp baking powder

75 g/2¾ oz caster sugar

50 g/1¾ oz dried apple, chopped

75 g/2¾ oz raisins

150 ml/5 fl oz sweet cider

1 egg, beaten

175 g/6 oz raspberries

1 Grease a 20-cm/8-inch cake tin with a little butter and line with baking paper.

2 Sieve the flour and baking powder into a large mixing bowl and rub in the butter with your fingertips until the mixture resembles fine breadcrumbs.

3 Stir in the caster sugar, dried apple and raisins.

4 Pour in the sweet cider and egg and mix together until thoroughly blended. Stir in the raspberries very gently so that they do not break up.

5 Pour the mixture into the prepared cake tin.

6 Bake in a preheated oven, 190°C/375°F/Gas Mark 5, for about 40 minutes, until risen and lightly golden.

7 Leave the cake to cool in the tin for 10 minutes, then turn out on to a wire rack to cool. Leave until completely cold before serving.

rich fruit cake

serves four

1 tbsp butter, for greasing

175 g/6 oz stoned chopped
   unsweetened dried dates

125 g/4½ oz no-soak dried
   prunes, chopped

200 ml/7 fl oz unsweetened
   orange juice

2 tbsp black treacle

1 tsp finely grated lemon rind

1 tsp finely grated orange rind

225 g/8 oz wholemeal
   self-raising flour

1 tsp mixed spice

125 g/4½ oz seedless raisins

125 g/4½ oz sultanas

125 g/4½ oz currants

125 g/4½ oz dried cranberries

3 large eggs, separated

TO DECORATE

1 tbsp apricot jam, warmed

icing sugar, for dusting

175 g/6 oz sugarpaste

strips of orange rind

strips of lemon rind

1 Grease a deep 20.5-cm/8-inch cake tin with the butter and line with baking paper. Place the dates and prunes in a saucepan over a low heat, pour over the orange juice and simmer for 10 minutes. Remove from the heat and beat into a purée. Stir in the treacle and rinds and set aside to cool.

2 Sift the flour and spice into a bowl, adding any bran that remains in the sieve. Add the dried fruits. When the date and prune mixture is cool, whisk in the egg yolks. In a separate bowl, whisk the egg whites until stiff. Add the fruit mixture to the dry ingredients and mix.

3 Gently fold in the egg whites. Transfer to the prepared tin and bake in a preheated oven, 160°C/325°F/Gas Mark 3, for 1½ hours. Leave to cool in the tin.

4 Turn the cake out and brush the top with apricot jam. Dust the work surface with icing sugar and roll out the sugarpaste thinly. Lay the sugarpaste over the top of the cake and trim the edges. Decorate with strips of orange and lemon rind.

carrot & ginger cake

serves ten

1 tbsp butter, for greasing

225 g/8 oz plain flour

1 tsp baking powder

1 tsp bicarbonate of soda

2 tsp ground ginger

½ tsp salt

175 g/6 oz light muscovado sugar

225 g/8 oz carrots, grated

2 pieces of chopped stem ginger

25 g/1 oz grated fresh root ginger

60 g/2¼ oz seedless raisins

2 eggs, beaten

3 tbsp corn oil

juice of 1 orange

FROSTING

225 g/8 oz low-fat soft cheese

4 tbsp icing sugar

1 tsp vanilla essence

TO DECORATE

grated carrot

finely chopped stem ginger

ground ginger

1 Grease a 20.5-cm/8-inch round cake tin with the butter and line with baking paper.

2 Sift the flour, baking powder, bicarbonate of soda, ground ginger and salt into a bowl. Stir in the sugar, carrots, stem and root ginger and raisins. In a separate bowl, beat the eggs, oil and orange juice together. Pour into the dry ingredients and mix.

3 Spoon the mixture into the cake tin and bake in a preheated oven, 180°C/350°F/Gas Mark 4, for 1–1¼ hours, until firm to the touch, or until a metal skewer inserted into the centre of the cake comes out clean. Leave in the tin to cool.

4 To make the frosting, place the soft cheese in a bowl and beat to soften. Sift in the icing sugar and add the vanilla essence. Mix well.

5 Turn the cake out and smooth the frosting over the top. Decorate with carrot and ginger and serve.

strawberry roulade

serves eight

3 large eggs

125 g/4½ oz caster sugar

125 g/4½ oz plain flour

1 tbsp hot water

FILLING

200 ml/7 fl oz low-fat fromage frais

1 tsp almond essence

225 g/8 oz small strawberries

TO DECORATE

1 tbsp toasted flaked almonds

1 tsp icing sugar

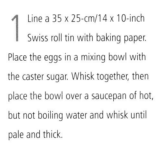

1 Line a 35 x 25-cm/14 x 10-inch Swiss roll tin with baking paper. Place the eggs in a mixing bowl with the caster sugar. Whisk together, then place the bowl over a saucepan of hot, but not boiling water and whisk until pale and thick.

2 Remove the bowl from the saucepan. Sieve in the flour and fold into the egg mixture with the hot water. Pour the mixture into the prepared tin and bake in a preheated oven, 220°C/425°F/Gas Mark 7, for 8–10 minutes, until golden and set.

3 Remove from the oven and transfer the roulade to a sheet of baking paper. Peel off the lining paper and roll up the sponge tightly along with the baking paper. Wrap in a tea towel and leave to cool.

4 To make the filling, mix together the fromage frais and almond essence. Reserve a few strawberries for decoration, then wash, hull and slice the remainder. Leave the fromage frais and strawberries to chill in the refrigerator until required.

5 Unroll the sponge, spread the fromage frais over the sponge and sprinkle with sliced strawberries. Roll the sponge up and transfer to a serving plate. Sprinkle with almonds and dust with icing sugar. Decorate with the reserved strawberries.

orange & almond cake

serves eight

1 tbsp butter, for greasing

4 eggs, separated

125 g/4½ oz caster sugar

finely grated rind and juice of
    2 oranges

finely grated rind and juice of
    1 lemon

125 g/4½ oz ground almonds

2½ tbsp self-raising flour

ORANGE-CINNAMON CREAM

200 ml/7 fl oz whipping cream

1 tsp ground cinnamon

2 tsp caster sugar

TO DECORATE

25 g/1 oz toasted flaked almonds

icing sugar, for dusting

VARIATION

You could serve this cake with a syrup. Boil the juice and grated rind of 2 oranges with 75 g/2¾ oz caster sugar and 2 tablespoons of water for 5–6 minutes, until slightly thickened. Stir in 1 tablespoon orange liqueur before serving.

1 Grease the base of an 18-cm/ 7-inch round deep cake tin with the butter and line with baking paper.

2 Cream the egg yolks and sugar in a bowl until the mixture is pale and thick. Whisk half of the orange rind and all of the lemon rind into the egg mixture.

COOK'S TIP

When whipping cream, chill the bowl, whisk and cream before starting. Whisk briskly until it starts to thicken and then more slowly until soft peaks form.

3 Mix the orange and lemon juice with the ground almonds and stir into the egg mixture. The mixture will be quite runny. Fold in the flour.

4 Whisk the egg whites until stiff, then gently fold them into the egg mixture.

5 Pour the mixture into the prepared tin and bake in a preheated oven, 180°C/350°F/Gas Mark 4, for 35–40 minutes, until golden and springy to the touch. Leave to cool in the tin for 10 minutes, then turn out and leave to cool completely.

6 Whip the cream until soft peaks form. Stir in the remaining orange rind, cinnamon and sugar. When the cake is cold, cover with the almonds, dust with icing sugar and serve with the orange-cinnamon cream.

coconut cake

serves six–eight

100 g/3½ oz butter, diced, plus
  extra for greasing

225 g/8 oz self-raising flour

pinch of salt

100 g/3½ oz demerara sugar

100 g/3½ oz desiccated coconut,
  plus extra for sprinkling

2 eggs, beaten

4 tbsp milk

2 Sieve the flour and salt into a
  mixing bowl and rub in the butter
with your fingertips until the mixture
resembles fine breadcrumbs.

1 Grease a 900-g/2-lb loaf tin with
  butter and line the base with
baking paper.

3 Stir in the sugar, coconut, eggs
  and milk and mix to a soft
dropping consistency.

4 Spoon the mixture into the
  prepared loaf tin and level the
surface with a palette knife. Bake in
a preheated oven, 160°C/325°F/
Gas Mark 3, for 30 minutes.

5 Remove the cake from the oven
  and sprinkle with the extra
coconut. Return to the oven and cook
for a further 30 minutes, until well
risen and golden and a fine metal
skewer inserted into the centre
comes out clean.

6 Leave the cake to cool in the
  tin for 10 minutes. Turn it out
and transfer to a wire rack to cool
completely before serving.

almond slices

1 Beat the eggs together in a bowl and set aside.

2 Place the ground almonds, dried milk, sugar and saffron in a large mixing bowl and mix well.

3 Melt the butter in a small saucepan over a low heat. Pour the melted butter over the dry ingredients and mix well until thoroughly blended.

4 Add the reserved beaten eggs to the mixture and mix well.

5 Spread the mixture in a shallow 15–20-cm/7–9-inch ovenproof dish and bake in a preheated oven,

COOK'S TIP
These almond slices are best eaten hot, but they may also be served cold. They can be made a day or even a week in advance and re-heated. They also freeze beautifully.

160°C/ 325°F/Gas Mark 3, for 45 minutes, or until a fine metal skewer inserted into the centre of the cake comes out clean.

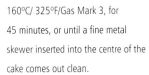

6 Cut the almond cake into 8 slices. Decorate the almond slices with flaked almonds and transfer to serving plates. Serve hot or cold.

pear & ginger cake

serves six

200 g/7 oz unsalted butter, softened, plus extra for greasing

175 g/6 oz caster sugar

175 g/6 oz self-raising flour

3 tsp ground ginger

3 eggs, beaten

450 g/1 lb pears, peeled, cored and thinly sliced, then brushed with lemon juice

1 tbsp soft brown sugar

ice cream or double cream, whipped lightly, to serve (optional)

COOK'S TIP

Soft brown sugar is often known as Barbados sugar. It is a darker form of soft light brown sugar. If the sugar has become hard in the store cupboard, do not throw it away. Wrap the package in a clean, damp tea towel and heat in the microwave on Medium for 1–2 minutes, until it begins to soften.

1 Lightly grease a deep 20-cm/8-inch cake tin with butter and line the base with baking paper.

2 Place 175 g/6 oz of the butter and the caster sugar in a bowl. Sieve in the flour and ground ginger and add the eggs. Beat well with a whisk until smooth.

3 Spoon the cake mixture into the prepared tin and level out the surface with a palette knife.

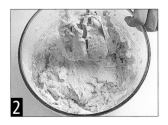

4 Arrange the pear slices over the cake mixture. Sprinkle with the brown sugar and dot with the remaining butter.

5 Bake in a preheated oven, 180°C/350°F/Gas Mark 4, for 35–40 minutes, or until the cake is golden and feels springy to the touch.

6 Serve the pear and ginger cake warm, with ice cream or whipped cream, if you wish.

VARIATION

For a different flavour, substitute 2 teaspoons ground cinnamon for the ground ginger and use vanilla sugar instead of plain.

coffee streusel cake

serves eight

100 g/3½ oz butter, melted and
    cooled, plus extra for greasing

275 g/9½ oz plain flour

1 tbsp baking powder

75 g/2¾ oz caster sugar

150 ml/5 fl oz milk

2 eggs

2 tbsp instant coffee mixed with
    1 tbsp boiling water

50 g/1¾ oz almonds, chopped

icing sugar, for dusting

TOPPING

75 g/2¾ oz self-raising flour

75 g/2¾ oz demerara sugar

2 tbsp butter, diced

1 tsp ground mixed spice

1 tbsp water

1 Grease a 23-cm/9-inch loose-bottomed round cake tin with the butter and line with baking paper. Sieve the flour and baking powder together into a large mixing bowl, then stir in the caster sugar.

2 Whisk the milk, eggs, melted butter and coffee mixture together and pour on to the dry ingredients. Add the chopped almonds and mix lightly together. Spoon the mixture into the prepared tin.

3 To make the topping, mix the self-raising flour and demerara sugar together.

4 Rub in the butter with your fingertips until the mixture resembles breadcrumbs. Sprinkle in the mixed spice and water and bring the mixture together into loose crumbs. Sprinkle the topping evenly over the surface of the cake mixture in the tin.

5 Bake in a preheated oven, 190°C/375°F/Gas Mark 5, for about 1 hour. If the topping starts to brown too quickly, cover loosely with foil. Leave to cool in the tin. Turn out, dust with icing sugar and serve.

gingerbread

makes twelve

150 g/5½ oz butter, plus extra
    for greasing

175 g/6 oz soft brown sugar

2 tbsp black treacle

225 g/8 oz plain flour

1 tsp baking powder

2 tsp bicarbonate of soda

2 tsp ground ginger

150 ml/5 fl oz milk

1 egg, beaten

2 eating apples, peeled, chopped,
    and coated with lemon juice to
    prevent them browning

VARIATION

If you enjoy the flavour of
ginger, try adding 25 g/1 oz
finely chopped stem ginger to
the mixture in step 3.

---

1 Grease a 23-cm/9-inch square
cake tin with a little butter and
line with baking paper.

2 Melt the butter, sugar and treacle
in a saucepan over a low heat,
then leave the mixture to cool.

3 Sieve the flour, baking powder,
bicarbonate of soda and ground
ginger into a mixing bowl.

4 Stir in the milk, beaten egg and
cooled butter and treacle mixture,
followed by the chopped apples.

5 Stir together gently, then pour the
mixture into the prepared tin and
level the surface with a palette knife.

6 Bake in a preheated oven,
160°C/325°F/Gas Mark 3, for
30–35 minutes, until the cake has
risen and a fine metal skewer inserted
into the centre comes out clean.

7 Leave the ginger cake to cool
in the tin, then turn out and cut
into 12 bars.

cherry scones

makes eight

6 tbsp butter, diced, plus extra
    for greasing

225 g/8 oz self-raising flour, plus
    extra for dusting

1 tbsp caster sugar

pinch of salt

40 g/1½ oz glacé cherries, chopped

40 g/1½ oz sultanas

1 egg, beaten

50 ml/2 fl oz milk

COOK'S TIP

These scones will freeze
very successfully, but they are
best thawed and eaten
within 1 month.

1 Lightly grease a baking tray with a little butter.

2 Sieve the flour, sugar and salt into a mixing bowl and rub in the butter with your fingertips until the mixture resembles breadcrumbs.

3 Stir in the glacé cherries and sultanas, then add the egg.

4 Reserve 1 tablespoon of the milk for glazing, then add the remainder to the mixture. Bring together to form a soft dough.

5 Roll out the scone dough on a lightly floured work surface to a thickness of 2 cm/¾ inch, then cut out 8 scones using a 5-cm/2-inch cutter.

6 Place the scones on the prepared baking tray and brush the tops with the reserved milk.

7 Bake the scones in a preheated oven, 220°C/425°F/Gas Mark 7, for 8–10 minutes, or until they are golden brown.

8 Transfer the scones to a wire rack and leave to cool slightly. Serve split in half and spread with butter.

treacle scones

makes eight

6 tbsp butter, diced, plus extra
    for greasing

225 g/8 oz self-raising flour, plus
    extra for dusting

1 tbsp caster sugar

pinch of salt

1 eating apple, peeled, cored
    and chopped

1 egg, beaten

2 tbsp black treacle

5 tbsp milk

1 Lightly grease a baking tray with a little butter.

2 Sieve the flour, sugar and salt into a mixing bowl.

3 Add the butter and rub it in with your fingertips until the mixture resembles fine breadcrumbs.

4 Stir the apple into the mixture until thoroughly blended.

5 Mix the beaten egg, treacle and milk together in a jug. Add to the dry ingredients and bring together to form a soft dough.

6 Roll out the scone dough on a lightly floured work surface to a thickness of 2cm/¾ inch, then stamp out 8 scones with a 5-cm/2-inch cutter.

7 Arrange the scones on the prepared baking tray and bake in a preheated oven, 220°C/425°F/Gas Mark 7, for 8–10 minutes.

8 Transfer the scones to a wire rack and leave to cool slightly. Serve split in half and spread with butter.

apple shortcakes

makes four

2 tbsp butter, diced, plus extra
  for greasing

150 g/5½ oz plain flour, plus extra
  for dusting

½ tsp salt

1 tsp baking powder

1 tbsp caster sugar

50 ml/2 fl oz milk

icing sugar, for dusting (optional)

FILLING

3 eating apples, peeled, cored
  and sliced

100 g/3½ oz caster sugar

1 tbsp lemon juice

1 tsp ground cinnamon

300 ml/10 fl oz water

150 ml/5 fl oz double cream,
  whipped lightly

1 Grease a baking tray with butter.
  Sieve the flour, salt and baking
powder into a bowl. Stir in the sugar.
Rub in the butter with your fingers until
the mixture resembles breadcrumbs.

2 Pour in the milk and bring
  together to form a soft dough.
Knead lightly on a lightly floured

surface, then roll out to a thickness of
1 cm/½ inch. Stamp out 4 rounds using
a 5-cm/2-inch cutter. Transfer the
rounds to the prepared baking tray.

3 Bake in a preheated oven, 220°C/
  425°F/Gas Mark 7, for about
15 minutes, until the shortcakes are
well risen and browned. Leave to cool.

4 To make the filling, place the
  apple slices, sugar, lemon juice
and cinnamon in a saucepan. Add the
water, bring to the boil and simmer,
uncovered, for 5–10 minutes, until the
apples are tender. Leave to cool a little,
then remove the apples from the pan.

5 To serve, split the shortcakes in
  half. Place each bottom half on a
serving plate and spoon on apple
slices and cream. Place the other half
of the shortcake on top. Serve dusted
with icing sugar, if wished.

sugar-topped blackberry & apple cake

serves ten

1 tbsp butter, for greasing

350 g/12 oz cooking apples

3 tbsp lemon juice

300 g/10½ oz wholemeal
self-raising flour

½ tsp baking powder

1 tsp ground cinnamon, plus extra
for dusting

175 g/6 oz prepared blackberries,
thawed if frozen, plus extra
to decorate

175 g/6 oz light muscovado sugar

1 egg, beaten

200 ml/7 fl oz low-fat fromage frais

55 g/2 oz white or brown sugar
cubes, crushed lightly

sliced eating apple, to decorate

VARIATION

Try replacing the blackberries
with blueberries. Use canned or
frozen blueberries if fresh
fruit is unavailable.

1 Grease a 900-g/2-lb loaf tin with butter and line with baking paper. Core, peel and finely dice the apples. Place them in a saucepan with the lemon juice, bring to the boil, cover and simmer for 10 minutes, until soft. Beat into a purée, then leave to cool.

2 Sift the flour, baking powder and cinnamon into a bowl, adding any bran that remains in the sieve. Stir in 115 g/4 oz of the blackberries and the sugar.

3 Make a well in the centre of the ingredients and add the egg, fromage frais and cooled apple purée. Mix until thoroughly blended. Spoon the mixture into the prepared loaf tin and level the top with a palette knife.

4 Sprinkle with the remaining blackberries, pressing them down into the cake mixture, and top with the crushed sugar cubes. Bake in a preheated oven, 190°C/375°F/Gas Mark 5, for 40–45 minutes. Leave to cool in the tin.

5 Turn the cake out and peel away the lining paper. Serve dusted with cinnamon and decorated with blackberries and apple slices.

spicy bread

makes one loaf

2 tbsp butter, diced, plus extra
   for greasing

225 g/8 oz self-raising flour, plus
   extra for dusting

100 g/3½ oz plain flour

1 tsp baking powder

¼ tsp salt

¼ tsp cayenne pepper

2 tsp curry powder

2 tsp poppy seeds

150 ml/5 fl oz milk

1 egg, beaten

COOK'S TIP

If the bread looks as though it is
browning too much, cover it with
foil for the remainder of the
cooking time.

1 Lightly grease a baking tray with a little butter.

2 Sieve the self-raising flour and the plain flour into a mixing bowl along with the baking powder, salt, cayenne pepper, curry powder and poppy seeds.

3 Rub in the butter with your fingertips until the mixture resembles breadcrumbs.

4 Add the milk and beaten egg and bring together with your fingers to form a soft dough.

5 Turn the dough out on to a lightly floured work surface, then knead lightly for a few minutes.

6 Shape the dough into a round about 5 cm/2 inches deep, and mark a cross on top with a sharp knife.

7 Bake in a preheated oven, 190°C/375°F/Gas Mark 5, for 45 minutes.

8 Remove the bread from the oven, transfer to a wire rack and leave to cool slightly. Serve the bread cut into chunks or slices.

cheese & ham loaf

makes one loaf

6 tbsp butter, diced, plus extra
   for greasing

225 g/8 oz self-raising flour

1 tsp salt

2 tsp baking powder

1 tsp paprika

125 g/4½ oz mature cheese, grated

75 g/2¾ oz smoked ham, chopped

2 eggs, beaten

150 ml/5 fl oz milk

COOK'S TIP

This tasty bread is best eaten on
the day it is made, as it does not
keep for very long.

1 Grease a 450-g/1-lb loaf tin with
a little butter and line the base
with baking paper.

2 Sieve the flour, salt, baking
powder and paprika into a large
mixing bowl.

3 Add the butter and rub it in with
your fingertips until the mixture
resembles fine breadcrumbs. Stir in the
cheese and ham.

4 Add the beaten eggs and milk to
the dry ingredients in the bowl
and mix well.

5 Spoon the cheese and ham
mixture into the prepared loaf tin.

6 Bake in a preheated oven,
180°C/350°F/Gas Mark 4, for
about 1 hour, or until the loaf is
well risen.

7 Leave the bread to cool in the tin,
then turn out and transfer to a
wire rack to cool completely.

8 Cut the bread into thick slices
to serve.

sun-dried tomato rolls

makes eight

100 g/3½ oz butter, melted and
   cooled slightly, plus extra
   for greasing
225 g/8 oz strong white bread flour,
   plus extra for dusting
½ tsp salt
1 sachet easy-blend dried yeast
3 tbsp milk, warmed
2 eggs, beaten
50 g/1¾ oz sun-dried tomatoes in
   oil, drained and finely chopped
milk, for brushing

VARIATION

Add some finely chopped
anchovies or olives to the dough
in step 5 for extra flavour,
if you wish.

---

1 Lightly grease a baking tray with
a little butter.

2 Sieve the flour and salt into a
large mixing bowl. Stir in the
yeast, then pour in the melted butter,
milk and beaten eggs. Bring together
with your fingers to form a dough.

3 Turn the dough out on to a lightly
floured work surface and knead
for about 5 minutes, until smooth.
Alternatively, use an electric mixer
with a dough hook.

4 Place the dough in a greased
bowl, cover and leave to rise in a
warm place for 1–1½ hours, or until it
has doubled in size.

5 Knead the dough for 2–3 minutes
to knock it back, then knead in
the sun-dried tomatoes, sprinkling the
work surface with a little extra flour
because the tomatoes are quite oily.

6 Divide the dough into 8 even-
sized balls and place them on the
prepared baking tray. Cover and leave
to rise for about 30 minutes, or until
the rolls have doubled in size.

7 Brush the rolls with milk and bake
in a preheated oven, 230°C/
450°F/Gas Mark 8, for 10–15 minutes,
or until they are golden brown.

8 Transfer the tomato rolls to a wire
rack and leave to cool slightly
before serving.

garlic bread rolls

makes eight

1 tbsp butter, for greasing

12 cloves garlic,

350 ml/12 fl oz milk, plus extra
for brushing

450 g/1 lb strong white bread flour,
plus extra for dusting

1 tsp salt

1 sachet easy-blend dried yeast

1 tbsp dried mixed herbs

2 tbsp sunflower oil

1 egg, beaten

milk, for brushing

rock salt, for sprinkling

1 Lightly grease a baking tray with
the butter.

2 Peel the garlic cloves and place
them in a saucepan with the milk.
Bring to the boil and simmer gently
over a low heat for 15 minutes. Leave
to cool slightly, then place in a food
processor and process into a purée.

3 Sieve the flour and salt into a
large mixing bowl and stir in the
dried yeast and mixed herbs.

4 Add the garlic-flavoured milk,
sunflower oil and beaten egg to
the dry ingredients, then mix well and
bring together with your fingers to
form a dough.

5 Turn the dough out on to a
lightly floured work surface and
knead lightly for a few minutes until
smooth and soft.

6 Place the dough in a lightly
greased bowl, cover and leave to
rise in a warm place for about 1 hour,
or until doubled in size.

7 Knead the dough for 2 minutes to
knock it back. Divide into 8 rolls
and place on the prepared baking tray.
Score the top of each roll with a knife,
cover and leave for 15 minutes.

8 Brush the rolls with milk and
sprinkle rock salt over the top.

9 Bake in a preheated oven,
220°C/425°F/Gas Mark 7, for
15–20 minutes. Transfer to a wire rack
and leave to cool before serving.

mini focaccia

serves four

2 tbsp olive oil, plus extra
    for greasing

350 g/12 oz strong white flour, plus
    extra for dusting

½ tsp salt

1 sachet easy-blend dried yeast

250 ml/9 fl oz hand-hot water

100 g/3½ oz stoned green or black
    olives, halved

TOPPING

2 red onions, sliced

2 tbsp olive oil

1 tsp sea salt

1 tbsp thyme leaves

1 Lightly oil several baking trays. Sieve the flour and salt into a large mixing bowl, then stir in the yeast. Pour in the olive oil and water and bring together with your fingers to form a dough.

2 Turn the dough out on to a lightly floured work surface and knead for about 5 minutes. Alternatively, use an electric mixer with a dough hook.

3 Place the dough in a greased bowl, cover and leave in a warm place for about 1–1½ hours, or until it has doubled in size.

4 Knead the dough for 1–2 minutes to knock it back, then knead half of the olives into the dough. Divide the dough into quarters, then shape the quarters into rounds. Place them on the baking trays and push your fingers into the dough rounds to create a dimpled effect.

5 To make the topping, sprinkle the red onions and remaining olives over the rounds. Drizzle the oil over the top and sprinkle with the sea salt and thyme leaves. Cover and leave to rise for 30 minutes.

6 Bake in a preheated oven, 190°C/375°F/Gas Mark 5, for 20–25 minutes, or until the focaccia are golden.

7 Transfer to a wire rack and leave to cool before serving.

VARIATION

Use this quantity of dough
to make 1 large focaccia,
if you wish.

soda bread

makes one loaf

1 tbsp butter, for greasing

300 g/10½ oz plain white flour, plus extra for dusting

300 g/10½ oz plain wholemeal flour

2 tsp baking powder

1 tsp bicarbonate of soda

2 tbsp caster sugar

1 tsp salt

1 egg, beaten

425 ml/15 fl oz natural yogurt

VARIATION

For a fruity version of this soda bread, add 125 g/4½ oz raisins to the dry ingredients in step 2.

---

1 Grease a baking tray with the butter and dust with flour.

2 Sieve the flours, baking powder, bicarbonate of soda, sugar and salt into a large bowl and add any bran remaining in the sieve.

3 In a jug, beat together the egg and yogurt and pour the mixture into the dry ingredients. Mix well, bringing the ingredients together to form a soft, sticky dough.

4 Knead the dough on a lightly floured work surface for a few minutes until smooth, then shape it into a large round about 5 cm/ 2 inches deep.

5 Transfer the dough to the baking tray. Mark a cross shape on top with a sharp knife.

6 Bake in a preheated oven, 190°C/ 375°F/Gas Mark 5, for about 40 minutes, or until the soda bread is golden brown all over.

7 Transfer the loaf to a wire rack and leave to cool completely. Cut into slices to serve.

Biscuits

Nothing can compare with a home-made biscuit for bringing a touch of pleasure to a coffee break or tea-time. This selection of delicious biscuits and after-dinner treats will tantalize your taste buds and keep you coming back for more.

Tasty biscuits, such as Citrus Crescents, Meringue Creams, Rock Drops, and Gingernuts, are quick, easy and satisfying to make. You can easily vary any of the ingredients listed to suit your taste – the possibilities for inventiveness when making biscuits are endless and this chapter shows you how.

savoury curried biscuits

makes forty

100 g/3½ oz butter, softened, plus
    extra for greasing

100 g/3½ oz plain flour, plus extra
    for dusting

1 tsp salt

2 tsp curry powder

100 g/3½ oz Cheshire
    cheese, grated

100 g/3½ oz freshly grated
    Parmesan cheese

COOK'S TIP

These biscuits can be stored for
several days in an airtight tin or
plastic container.

1 Lightly grease about 4 baking
trays with a little butter.

2 Sieve the flour and salt into a
mixing bowl.

3 Stir in the curry powder and the
grated Cheshire and Parmesan
cheeses. Rub in the butter with your
fingertips, then bring the mixture
together to form a soft dough.

4 Roll out the dough thinly on a
lightly floured surface.

5 Stamp out 40 biscuits using a
5-cm/2-inch round biscuit cutter.

6 Arrange the biscuits on the
prepared baking trays.

7 Bake in a preheated oven,
180°C/350°F/Gas Mark 4, for
10–15 minutes, until golden brown.

8 Leave the curried biscuits to cool
slightly on the baking trays, then
carefully transfer them to a wire rack to
cool. Leave until completely cold and
crisp, then serve.

3

4

5

rosemary biscuits

makes twenty-five

50 g/1¾ oz butter, softened, plus
 extra for greasing

50 g/1¾ oz caster sugar

grated rind of 1 lemon

4 tbsp lemon juice

1 egg, separated

2 tsp finely chopped fresh rosemary

200 g/7 oz plain flour, sieved, plus
 extra for dusting

caster sugar, for sprinkling (optional)

VARIATION

In place of the fresh rosemary,
use 1½ teaspoons of dried
rosemary, if you wish.

---

1 Lightly grease 2 baking trays with
 a little butter.

2 Cream the butter and sugar
 together in a large mixing bowl
until pale and fluffy.

3 Add the lemon rind and juice and
 the egg yolk and beat until the
mixture is thoroughly blended. Stir in
the chopped fresh rosemary.

4 Mix in the sieved flour and bring
 together to form a soft dough.
Wrap in clingfilm and chill in the
refrigerator for 30 minutes.

5 Roll out the dough thinly on a
 lightly floured surface. Stamp out
about 25 circles with a 6-cm/2½-inch
biscuit cutter. Arrange the dough circles
on the prepared baking trays.

6 Lightly whisk the egg white in a
 small bowl. Gently brush the egg
white over the surface of each biscuit,
then sprinkle with a little caster sugar,
if you wish.

7 Bake in a preheated oven,
 180°C/350°F/Gas Mark 4, for
about 15 minutes.

8 Transfer the biscuits to a wire rack
 and leave to cool before serving.

cheese sablés

makes thirty-five

150 g/5½ oz butter, diced, plus
    extra for greasing
150 g/5½ oz plain flour, plus extra
    for dusting
150 g/5½ oz mature cheese, grated
1 egg yolk
sesame seeds, for sprinkling

COOK'S TIP

Cut out any shape you like for
your savoury biscuits. Children
will enjoy them cut into animal
shapes or other fun designs.

---

1 Lightly grease several baking trays
    with a little butter.

2 Mix the flour and cheese together
    in a bowl.

3 Add the butter to the cheese
    and flour mixture and rub in with
your fingertips until the mixture
resembles breadcrumbs.

4 Stir in the egg yolk and mix to
    form a dough. Wrap in clingfilm.
Chill in the refrigerator for 30 minutes.

5 Roll out the dough thinly on a
    lightly floured work surface.
Stamp out rounds with a 6-cm/2½-inch
biscuit cutter, re-rolling the trimmings
to make 35 biscuits.

6 Place the rounds on to the
    prepared baking trays and
sprinkle the sesame seeds over the
top of them.

7 Bake in a preheated oven,
    200°C/400°F/Gas Mark 6, for
20 minutes, until lightly golden.

8 Carefully transfer the cheese
    sablés to a wire rack and leave
to cool slightly before serving.

VARIATION

For a sweet variation of these
traditional French biscuits,
substitute the grated rind of
1 lemon for the cheese and stir in
125 g/4½ oz caster sugar at the
end of step 2. Beat the egg yolk
with 1 tablespoon brandy or rum
before adding it to the mixture.
Roll out the dough, stamp out
rounds and bake as above.

cheese & chive scones

makes ten

225 g/8 oz self-raising flour, plus
    extra for dusting

1 tsp powdered mustard

½ tsp cayenne pepper

½ tsp salt

100 g/3½ oz low-fat soft cheese
    with added herbs

2 tbsp snipped fresh chives, plus
    extra to garnish

100 ml/3½ fl oz skimmed milk, plus
    extra for brushing

55 g/2 oz reduced-fat mature
    Cheddar cheese, grated

low-fat soft cheese, to serve

1 Sift the flour, mustard, cayenne and salt into a large mixing bowl.

2 Add the soft cheese to the flour mixture and stir together until well blended, then stir in the snipped chives.

3 Make a well in the centre of the ingredients and gradually pour in the skimmed milk, stirring as you pour, bringing the mixture together to form a soft dough.

4 Turn the dough out on to a floured surface and knead lightly. Roll out to a thickness of 2 cm/¾ inch. Stamp out as many rounds as you can using a 5-cm/2-inch round pastry cutter. Transfer to a baking sheet.

5 Knead the dough trimmings together and roll out again. Stamp out more rounds – you should be able to make 10 scones in total.

6 Brush the scones with milk and sprinkle with the grated cheese. Bake in a preheated oven at 200°C/ 400°F/Gas Mark 6 for 15–20 minutes, until risen and golden. Transfer to a wire rack to cool. Serve warm with low-fat soft cheese, garnished with snipped chives.

cheese & mustard scones

makes eight

4 tbsp butter, diced, plus extra
    for greasing
225 g/8 oz self-raising flour, plus
    extra for dusting
1 tsp baking powder
125 g/4½ oz mature cheese, grated
1 tsp mustard powder
150 ml/5 fl oz milk, plus extra
    for brushing
salt and pepper

1 Lightly grease a baking tray with a little butter.

2 Sieve the flour, baking powder and a pinch of salt into a bowl. Rub in the butter with your fingers until the mixture resembles breadcrumbs.

3 Stir in the grated cheese, mustard powder and enough milk to form a soft dough.

4 Knead the dough very lightly on a lightly floured work surface, then flatten it out with the palm of your hand to a depth of about 2.5 cm/1 inch.

5 Cut the dough into 8 wedges with a knife. Brush the wedges with a little milk and sprinkle with pepper to taste.

6 Bake in a preheated oven, 220°C/425°F/Gas Mark 7, for 10–15 minutes, until the scones are golden brown.

7 Transfer the cheese and mustard scones to a wire rack and leave to cool slightly before serving.

111

gingernuts

makes thirty

125 g/4½ oz butter, plus extra
    for greasing
350 g/12 oz self-raising flour
pinch of salt
200 g/7 oz caster sugar
1 tbsp ground ginger
1 tsp bicarbonate of soda
75 g/2¾ oz golden syrup
1 egg, beaten
1 tsp grated orange rind

COOK'S TIP
Store these biscuits in an
airtight container and eat
them within 1 week.

VARIATION
For less traditional, but equally
delicious biscuits, substitute
1 tablespoon mixed spice for the
ground ginger and 1 teaspoon
finely grated lemon rind for the
orange rind.

1   Lightly grease several baking trays with a little butter.

2   Sieve the flour, salt, sugar, ginger and bicarbonate of soda into a large mixing bowl.

3   Put the butter and golden syrup into a saucepan and place the saucepan over a very low heat until the butter has melted.

4   Remove the saucepan from the heat and leave the butter and syrup mixture to cool slightly, then pour it on to the dry ingredients.

5   Add the egg and orange rind and bring together to form a dough.

6   Using your hands, shape the dough into 30 even-sized balls.

7   Place the balls well apart on the prepared baking trays, then flatten them slightly with your fingers.

8   Bake in a preheated oven, 160°C/325°F/Gas Mark 3, for 15–20 minutes. Transfer the biscuits to a wire rack to cool before serving.

lemon jumbles

makes fifty

100 g/3½ oz butter, softened, plus
    extra for greasing
125 g/4½ oz caster sugar
grated rind of 1 lemon
1 egg, beaten
4 tbsp lemon juice
350 g/12 oz plain flour, plus extra
    for dusting
1 tsp baking powder
1 tbsp milk
icing sugar, for dredging

VARIATION
If you prefer, form the dough into other shapes – letters of the alphabet or geometric designs.

1 Lightly grease several baking trays with a little butter.

2 Cream the butter, caster sugar and lemon rind together in a mixing bowl until pale and fluffy.

3 Add the beaten egg and lemon juice, a little at a time, beating thoroughly after each addition.

4 Sieve the flour and baking powder into the mixture and mix until blended. Add the milk and bring together to form a soft dough.

5 Turn the dough out on to a lightly floured work surface and divide into about 50 equal-sized pieces.

6 Roll each piece into a sausage shape with your hands and bend into an 'S' shape.

7 Place the dough shapes on the prepared baking trays and bake in a preheated oven, 160°C/325°F/Gas Mark 3, for 15–20 minutes. Carefully transfer to a wire rack and leave to cool completely. Dredge with icing sugar to serve.

cinnamon & seed squares

makes twelve

250 g/9 oz butter, softened, plus
   extra for greasing
250 g/9 oz caster sugar
3 eggs, beaten
250 g/9 oz self-raising flour
½ tsp bicarbonate of soda
1 tbsp ground cinnamon
150 ml/5 fl oz soured cream
100 g/3½ oz sunflower seeds

COOK'S TIP

These moist squares will
freeze well and will keep for
up to 1 month.

1 Grease a 23-cm/9-inch square
cake tin with a little butter and
line the base with baking paper.

2 Cream the butter and caster sugar
together in a large mixing bowl
until light and fluffy.

3 Gradually add the beaten eggs to
the mixture, beating thoroughly
after each addition.

4 Sieve the self-raising flour,
bicarbonate of soda and ground
cinnamon into the creamed egg
mixture and fold in gently using a
metal spoon.

5 Spoon in the soured cream and
sunflower seeds and mix gently
until well blended.

6 Spoon the mixture into the
prepared cake tin and level the
surface with the back of a spoon or a
palette knife.

7 Bake in a preheated oven, 180°C/
350°F/Gas Mark 4, for about
45 minutes, until the surface is firm to
the touch.

8 Loosen the edges with a palette
knife, then turn out on to a wire
rack to cool completely. Slice into
12 squares to serve.

oat & raisin biscuits

makes ten

4 tbsp butter, plus extra for greasing

125 g/4½ oz caster sugar

1 egg, beaten

50 g/1¾ oz plain flour

½ tsp salt

½ tsp baking powder

175 g/6 oz rolled oats

125 g/4½ oz raisins

2 tbsp sesame seeds

COOK'S TIP

To enjoy these biscuits at their best, store them in an airtight container.

1 Lightly grease 2 baking trays with a little butter.

2 Cream the butter and sugar together in a large mixing bowl until light and fluffy.

3 Gradually add the beaten egg, beating thoroughly after each addition, until well blended.

4 Sieve the flour, salt and baking powder into the creamed mixture. Mix gently. Add the rolled oats, raisins and sesame seeds and mix together thoroughly.

5 Place 10 spoonfuls of the mixture on the prepared baking trays, spaced well apart to allow room to expand during cooking, and flatten them slightly with the back of a spoon.

6 Bake the biscuits in a preheated oven, 180°C/350°F/Gas Mark 4, for 15 minutes.

7 Leave the biscuits to cool slightly on the baking trays.

8 Carefully transfer the biscuits to a wire rack and leave to cool completely before serving.

hazelnut squares

makes sixteen

100 g/3½ oz butter, diced, plus
    extra for greasing

150 g/5½ oz plain flour

pinch of salt

1 tsp baking powder

150 g/5½ oz soft brown sugar

1 egg, beaten

4 tbsp milk

100 g/3½ oz hazelnuts, halved

demerara sugar, for
    sprinkling (optional)

1 Grease a 23-cm/9-inch square cake tin with a little butter and line the base with baking paper.

2 Sieve the flour, salt and baking powder into a large mixing bowl.

3 Add the butter and rub in with your fingertips until the mixture resembles fine breadcrumbs. Add the soft brown sugar to the mixture and stir to blend.

4 Add the beaten egg, milk and halved hazelnuts to the dry ingredients and stir well until thoroughly blended and the mixture has a soft consistency.

5 Spoon the mixture into the prepared cake tin and level the surface with a palette knife. Sprinkle with demerara sugar, if you wish.

6 Bake in a preheated oven, 180°C/350°F/Gas Mark 4, for about 25 minutes, or until the surface is firm to the touch.

7 Leave to cool in the tin for about 10 minutes, then loosen the edges with a palette knife and turn out on to a wire rack. Cut into 16 squares to serve.

VARIATION

For a coffee time biscuit, replace the milk with the same amount of cold strong black coffee – the stronger the better!

rock drops

makes eight

100 g/3½ oz butter, diced, plus
    extra for greasing

200 g/7 oz plain flour

2 tsp baking powder

75 g/2¾ oz demerara sugar

100 g/3½ oz sultanas

25 g/1 oz glacé cherries,
    chopped finely

1 egg, beaten

2 tbsp milk

COOK'S TIP

For convenience, prepare the dry
ingredients in advance and just
before cooking, stir in the liquid.

1 Lightly grease a baking tray with
a little butter.

2 Sieve the flour and baking
powder into a mixing bowl. Rub
in the butter with your fingertips until
the mixture resembles breadcrumbs.

3 Stir in the sugar, sultanas and
chopped glacé cherries.

4 Add the beaten egg and milk to
the mixture and bring together to
form a soft dough.

5 Spoon 8 mounds of the mixture
on to the prepared baking tray,
spaced well apart to allow room to
expand during cooking.

6 Bake in a preheated oven,
200°C/400°F/Gas Mark 6, for
15–20 minutes, until firm to the touch.

7 Remove the rock drops from the
baking tray. Serve piping hot from
the oven, or transfer to a wire rack and
leave to cool before serving.

2

5

coconut flapjacks

COOK'S TIP

The flapjacks are best stored in an airtight container and eaten within 1 week. They can also be frozen for up to 1 month.

VARIATION

For plain flapjacks, heat 3 tablespoons caster sugar, 3 tablespoons golden syrup and 115 g/4 oz butter in a saucepan over low heat until the butter has melted. Stir in 175 g/6 oz rolled oats or oat flakes until combined, then transfer to a greased baking tray and bake as above.

---

1 Grease a 30 x 23-cm/12 x 9-inch baking tray with a little butter.

2 Put the butter, demerara sugar and golden syrup into a large saucepan and place over a low heat until just melted.

3 Stir in the oats, desiccated coconut and glacé cherries and mix well until evenly combined.

4 Place the mixture on the prepared baking tray. Spread it evenly across the tray and level the surface by pressing with a palette knife.

5 Bake in a preheated oven, 170°C/325°F/Gas Mark 3, for about 30 minutes.

6 Remove from the oven and leave on the baking tray to cool for about 10 minutes.

7 Cut the flapjack into 16 pieces using a sharp knife.

8 Carefully transfer the flapjack squares to a wire rack and leave to cool completely.

citrus crescents

makes twenty-five

100 g/3½ oz butter, softened, plus
extra for greasing
75 g/2¾ oz caster sugar, plus extra
for dusting (optional)
1 egg, separated
200 g/7 oz plain flour, plus extra
for dusting
grated rind of 1 orange
grated rind of 1 lemon
grated rind of 1 lime
2–3 tbsp orange juice

1 Lightly grease 2 baking trays with a little butter.

2 Cream the butter and sugar together in a mixing bowl until light and fluffy, then gradually beat in the egg yolk.

3 Sieve the flour into the creamed mixture and mix until evenly blended. Add the orange, lemon and lime rinds to the mixture with enough orange juice to form a soft dough.

4 Roll the dough out on a lightly floured work surface. Stamp out rounds using a 7.5-cm/3-inch biscuit cutter. Make crescent shapes by cutting away a quarter of each round. Re-roll the trimmings to make 25 crescents.

5 Place the crescents on the prepared baking trays. Prick the surface of each crescent with a fork.

6 Lightly whisk the egg white in a small bowl and brush it over the biscuits. Dust with extra caster sugar, if you wish.

7 Bake in a preheated oven, 200°C/400°F/Gas Mark 6, for 12–15 minutes, then transfer the biscuits to a wire rack. Allow to cool completely and crispen before serving.

spiced biscuits

makes twelve

175 g/6 oz unsalted butter, plus
    extra for greasing

175 g/6 oz dark muscovado sugar

225 g/8 oz plain flour

a pinch of salt

½ tsp bicarbonate of soda

1 tsp ground cinnamon

½ tsp ground coriander

½ tsp ground nutmeg

¼ tsp ground cloves

2 tbsp dark rum

1 Lightly grease 2 baking trays with
a little butter.

2 Cream the butter and sugar
together in a mixing bowl until
light and fluffy.

3 Sieve the flour, salt, bicarbonate
of soda, cinnamon, coriander,
nutmeg and cloves into the butter and
sugar mixture.

COOK'S TIP

Use the back of a fork to flatten
the biscuits instead of a spoon,
to give them a textured surface.

4 Stir the dark rum into the creamed
mixture until blended.

5 Place 12 small mounds of the
mixture on to the baking trays
using 2 teaspoons. Space the mounds
well apart to allow room to expand
during cooking. Flatten each one
slightly with the back of a spoon.

6 Bake in a preheated oven,
180°C/350°F/Gas Mark 4, for
10–12 minutes, until golden.

7 Carefully transfer the biscuits to
wire racks to cool completely and
crispen before serving.

peanut butter cookies

makes twenty

125 g/4½ oz butter, softened, plus
extra for greasing

150 g/5½ oz chunky peanut butter

225 g/8 oz granulated sugar

1 egg, lightly beaten

150 g/5½ oz plain flour

½ tsp baking powder

pinch of salt

75 g/2¾ oz peanuts, chopped

COOK'S TIP

For a crunchy bite and sparkling
appearance, sprinkle the peanut
butter cookies with demerara
sugar before baking.

VARIATION

For a change, use light
muscovado sugar instead of
granulated and add 1 teaspoon
mixed spice with the flour and
baking powder.

1 Lightly grease 2 baking trays with a little butter.

2 Beat the butter and peanut butter together in a large mixing bowl.

3 Gradually add the granulated sugar and beat well.

4 Add the beaten egg, a little at a time, beating well after each addition until thoroughly blended.

5 Sieve the flour, baking powder and salt into the creamed peanut butter mixture.

6 Add the chopped peanuts and bring the mixture together with your fingers to form a soft dough. Wrap in clingfilm and chill in the refrigerator for about 30 minutes.

7 Form the dough into 20 balls and place them on the prepared baking trays, spaced well apart to allow room to expand during cooking. Flatten them slightly with your hand.

8 Bake in a preheated oven, 190°C/375°F/Gas Mark 5, for 15 minutes, until golden brown. Transfer the biscuits to a wire rack and leave to cool before serving.

shortbread fantails

makes eight

125 g/4½ oz butter, softened, plus
   extra for greasing
40 g/1½ oz granulated sugar
25 g/1 oz icing sugar
225 g/8 oz plain flour, plus extra
   for dusting
pinch of salt
2 tsp orange flower water
caster sugar, for sprinkling

1 Lightly grease a 20-cm/8-inch
shallow round cake tin with butter.

2 Cream the butter, granulated
sugar and icing sugar together in
a large mixing bowl until the mixture is
light and fluffy.

3 Sieve the flour and salt into
the mixture. Add the orange
flower water and bring together with
your fingers to form a soft dough.

4 Roll out the dough on a lightly
floured work surface into a
20-cm/8-inch round and place in the
prepared tin. Prick well and score into
8 triangles with a round-bladed knife.

5 Bake in a preheated oven,
150°C/300°F/Gas Mark 2, for
30–35 minutes, or until the shortbread
is crisp and pale golden.

6 Sprinkle with caster sugar, then
cut along the marked lines to
make the 8 fantails.

7 Leave the shortbread in the tin to
cool before serving. Store in an
airtight container.

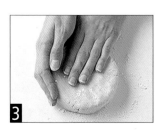

meringue creams

makes thirteen

4 egg whites
pinch of salt
125 g/4½ oz granulated sugar
125 g/4½ oz caster sugar
300 ml/10 fl oz double cream,
  whipped lightly, to serve

VARIATION
For a finer texture, replace
the granulated sugar with
caster sugar.

1 Line 3 large baking trays with baking paper.

2 Whisk the egg whites and salt together in a large bowl until they are stiff, using an electric whisk or a balloon whisk. (You should be able to turn the bowl upside down without any movement from the egg whites.)

3 Whisk in the granulated sugar, a little at a time; the meringue should start to look glossy.

4 Whisk in the caster sugar, a little at a time, whisking well after each addition until all the sugar has been incorporated and the meringue is thick, white and forms peaks.

5 Transfer the meringue mixture into a piping bag fitted with a 2-cm/¾-inch star nozzle. Pipe about 26 small whirls of meringue on to the prepared baking trays.

6 Bake in a preheated oven, 120°C/250°F/Gas Mark ½, for 1½ hours, or until the meringues are pale golden and can be easily lifted off the paper. Turn off the heat and leave them to cool in the oven overnight.

7 Just before serving, sandwich the meringue whirls together in pairs with the cream and arrange on a serving plate.

vanilla hearts

makes twelve

150 g/5½ oz butter, diced, plus
    extra for greasing
225 g/8 oz plain flour, plus extra
    for dusting
125 g/4½ oz caster sugar, plus extra
    for dusting
1 tsp vanilla essence

COOK'S TIP

Place a fresh vanilla pod in
your caster sugar and keep it
in a storage jar for several weeks
to give the sugar a delicious
vanilla flavour.

VARIATION

If you like, you could add a few
drops of red or pink food
colouring with the vanilla
essence and decorate the the
hearts with tiny silver, gold or
pink balls.

1 Lightly grease a baking tray with a little butter.

2 Sieve the flour into a large mixing bowl and rub in the butter with your fingertips until the mixture resembles fine breadcrumbs.

3 Stir in the caster sugar and vanilla essence and bring the mixture together with your hands to form a firm dough.

4 Roll out the dough on a lightly floured work surface to a thickness of 2.5 cm/1 inch. Stamp out 12 hearts with a heart-shaped biscuit cutter measuring about 5 cm/2 inches across and 2.5 cm/1 inch deep.

5 Arrange the hearts on the prepared baking tray. Bake in a preheated oven, 180°C/350°F/Gas Mark 4, for about 15–20 minutes, until light golden.

6 Transfer the vanilla hearts to a wire rack and leave to cool completely. Dust with a little caster sugar just before serving.

Starters & Snacks

With so many fresh ingredients readily
available, it is very easy to create some
deliciously different starters to make the perfect

introduction to any meal. The ideas in this chapter are an inspiration to cook

and a treat to eat, and they give an edge to the appetite that makes the main

course even more enjoyable. When choosing a starter, make sure that you

provide a good balance of flavours, colours and textures that offer variety and

contrast. Balance the nature of the recipes too – a rich main course is best

preceded by a light starter to stimulate the taste buds.

onion & mozzarella tarts

serves four

250 g/9 oz puff pastry, thawed
    if frozen

plain flour, for dusting

2 red onions

1 red pepper

8 cherry tomatoes, halved

100g/3½ oz mozzarella cheese,
    cut into chunks

8 fresh thyme sprigs

1 Roll out the pastry on a lightly floured work surface to make 4 squares, 7.5 cm/3 inches wide. Trim the edges of the pastry using a sharp knife, reserving the trimmings. Chill in the refrigerator for 30 minutes.

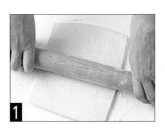

2 Place the pastry squares on a baking tray. Brush a little water around the edges of the pastry squares and use the reserved pastry trimmings to make a rim around each tart.

3 Cut the red onions into thin wedges and halve and deseed the red pepper.

4 Place the onions and red pepper in a grill pan. Cook under a preheated medium grill for 15 minutes, or until charred.

5 Place the roasted pepper halves in a polythene bag and leave to sweat for 10 minutes. When the pepper is cool enough to handle, peel off the skin and cut the flesh into strips.

6 Line the pastry squares with squares of foil. Bake in a preheated oven, 200°C/400°F/Gas Mark 6 for 10 minutes. Remove and discard the foil and bake the tart cases for a further 5 minutes.

7 Divide the onions, pepper strips, tomatoes and cheese between the tarts and sprinkle with fresh thyme.

8 Bake for a further 15 minutes, or until the pastry is golden. Transfer to warmed serving plates if serving hot, or to a wire rack to cool, if serving cold.

aubergine bake

serves four

3–4 tbsp olive oil

2 garlic cloves, crushed

2 large aubergines

100 g/3½ oz mozzarella cheese,
  sliced thinly

200 ml/7 fl oz passata

50 g/1¾ oz freshly grated
  Parmesan cheese

1 Heat 2 tablespoons of the olive oil in a large, heavy-based frying pan. Add the garlic and sauté over a low heat for 30 seconds.

2 Slice the aubergines lengthways. Add the slices to the frying pan and cook in the oil for 3–4 minutes on each side, or until tender (you may have to cook them in batches, so add the remaining oil as necessary).

3 Remove the aubergines with a slotted spoon and drain on kitchen paper.

4 Place a layer of aubergine slices in a shallow ovenproof dish. Cover the aubergines with a layer of mozzarella, then pour over a third of

the passata. Continue layering in the same order, finishing with a layer of passata on top.

5 Generously sprinkle the freshly grated Parmesan cheese evenly over the top of the dish and bake in a preheated oven, 200°C/400°F/Gas Mark 6, for about 25–30 minutes.

6 Transfer to serving plates and serve warm, or leave to cool, chill in the refrigerator and serve.

baked fennel

serves four

2 fennel bulbs

2 celery sticks, cut into 7.5-cm/
   3-inch pieces

6 sun-dried tomatoes, halved

200 ml/7 fl oz passata

2 tsp dried oregano

50 g/1¾ oz freshly grated
   Parmesan cheese

1 Trim the fennel using a sharp knife, discard any tough outer leaves and cut the bulbs into quarters.

2 Bring a large saucepan of water to the boil, add the fennel and celery and cook for 8–10 minutes, or until just tender. Remove with a slotted spoon and drain.

3 Place the fennel pieces, celery and sun-dried tomatoes in a large ovenproof dish.

4 Mix the passata and oregano in a bowl and pour the mixture over the vegetables in the dish.

5 Sprinkle the surface evenly with the Parmesan cheese and bake in a preheated oven, 190°C/375°F/Gas Mark 5, for 20 minutes, or until piping hot. Serve as a starter with fresh crusty bread or as a vegetable side dish.

cheese & onion pies

serves four

FILLING

3 tbsp vegetable oil

4 onions, sliced thinly

4 garlic cloves, crushed

4 tbsp finely chopped fresh parsley

75 g/2¾ oz mature cheese, grated

salt and pepper

PASTRY

175 g/6 oz plain flour, plus extra
for dusting

½ tsp salt

100 g/3½ oz butter, diced

3–4 tbsp water

COOK'S TIP

You can prepare the filling in
advance and store it in the
refrigerator until required.

VARIATION

Use red or white onions for an
extra sweet, mild flavour and
sprinkle with 1 teaspoon of sugar
5 minutes before the end of the
cooking time in step 1.

1 Heat the oil in a frying pan over a low heat. Add the onions and garlic and fry for 10–15 minutes, or until the onions are soft. Remove the pan from the heat, stir in the parsley and cheese and season to taste.

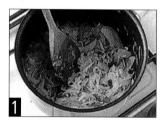

2 To make the pastry, sieve the flour and salt into a bowl. Rub in the butter with your fingertips until the mixture resembles fine breadcrumbs. Gradually stir in the water and bring together to form a dough.

3 Roll out the dough on a lightly floured work surface and divide it into 8 portions.

4 Roll out each portion into a 10-cm/4-inch round and use 4 of the rounds to line 4 individual tartlet tins. Fill each pie base with a quarter of the cheese and onion mixture.

5 Cover the pies with the remaining pastry rounds. Make a slit in the top of each pie with the point of a sharp knife to allow steam to escape during cooking, and press the edges of the pies firmly to seal them with the back of a teaspoon.

6 Bake in a preheated oven, 220°C/425°F/Gas Mark 7, for 20 minutes. Transfer the pies to warmed plates and serve.

stuffed tomatoes

serves six

6 large, firm tomatoes

4 tbsp unsalted butter

5 tbsp vegetable oil

1 medium onion, chopped finely

1 tsp finely chopped fresh
    root ginger

1 tsp crushed garlic

1 tsp pepper

1 tsp salt

½ tsp garam masala

450 g/1 lb minced lamb

1 fresh green chilli, deseeded and
    finely chopped

fresh coriander leaves

1 Slice the tops off the tomatoes and reserve, then scoop out the flesh. Grease an ovenproof dish with all of the butter and place the tomatoes in it.

2 Heat the oil in a saucepan over a medium heat, add the onion and fry until golden.

3 Reduce the heat and add the ginger, garlic, pepper, salt and garam masala. Stir-fry for 3–5 minutes.

4 Add the minced lamb and fry for 10–15 minutes, until browned.

5 Add the green chilli and fresh coriander leaves and stir-fry for a further 3–5 minutes.

6 Spoon the lamb mixture into the tomatoes and replace the tops. Bake in a preheated oven, 180°C/350°F/Gas Mark 4, for 15–20 minutes.

7 Transfer the tomatoes to serving plates and serve hot.

pasta-stuffed tomatoes

serves eight

5 tbsp extra virgin olive oil, plus
    extra for greasing

8 beef tomatoes or large
    round tomatoes

115 g/4 oz dried ditalini or other
    very small pasta shapes

8 black olives, stoned and
    finely chopped

2 tbsp finely chopped fresh basil

1 tbsp finely chopped fresh parsley

55 g/2 oz freshly grated
    Parmesan cheese

salt and pepper

fresh basil sprigs, to garnish

1 Brush a baking tray with olive oil. Slice the tops off the tomatoes and reserve to use as lids. If the tomatoes will not stand up, cut a thin slice off the bottom of each of them.

2 Scoop out the tomato pulp into a sieve using a teaspoon and leave to drain. Invert the tomato shells on kitchen paper, pat dry, then set aside.

3 Bring a large saucepan of lightly salted water to the boil. Add the pasta and 1 tablespoon of the remaining olive oil, bring back to a boil and cook for 8–10 minutes, or until tender but firm to the bite. Drain and set aside.

4 Put the olives, basil, parsley and Parmesan cheese into a large mixing bowl and stir in the drained tomato flesh. Add the pasta to the bowl. Stir in the remaining oil, mix together well and season to taste.

5 Spoon the pasta mixture into the tomato shells and replace the lids. Arrange the stuffed tomatoes on the prepared baking tray and bake in a preheated oven, 190°C/375°F/Gas Mark 5, for 15–20 minutes.

6 Remove the tomatoes from the oven. Set aside to cool slightly.

7 Arrange the tomatoes on a serving dish, garnish with basil sprigs and serve.

mexican-style pizzas

serves four

4 ready-made individual pizza bases

1 tbsp olive oil

200 g/7 oz canned chopped
  tomatoes with garlic and herbs

2 tbsp tomato purée

200 g/7 oz canned kidney beans,
  drained and rinsed

115 g/4 oz sweetcorn kernels,
  thawed if frozen

1–2 tsp chilli sauce

1 large red onion, shredded

100 g/3½ oz mature Cheddar
  cheese, grated

1 large, fresh green chilli, deseeded
  and sliced into rings

salt and pepper

COOK'S TIP

Serve a Mexican-style salad
with this pizza. Arrange sliced
tomatoes, fresh coriander leaves
and a few slices of a small,
ripe avocado on a platter.
Sprinkle with fresh lime juice
and coarse sea salt.

1 Arrange the ready-made pizza bases on a large baking tray and brush the surfaces lightly with the olive oil.

2 Mix the chopped tomatoes, tomato purée, kidney beans and sweetcorn together in a bowl and add chilli sauce to taste. Season with salt and pepper.

3 Spread the tomato and kidney bean mixture evenly over each of the pizza bases.

4 Top each pizza with shredded onion and sprinkle with some grated Cheddar cheese and a few slices of green chilli, to taste.

5 Bake in a preheated oven, 220°C/ 425°F/Gas Mark 7, for about 20 minutes, until the vegetables are tender, the cheese has melted and the base is crisp and golden.

6 Remove the pizzas from the baking tray and transfer to serving plates. Serve hot.

mini pizzas

serves eight

BASIC PIZZA DOUGH

2 tsp dried yeast

1 tsp sugar

250 ml/9 fl oz hand-hot water

350 g/12 oz strong plain flour, plus
   extra for dusting

1 tsp salt

1 tbsp olive oil, plus extra
   for brushing

TOPPING

2 courgettes

100 ml/3½ fl oz passata

75 g/2¾ oz pancetta, diced

50 g/1¾ oz black olives, stoned
   and chopped

1 tbsp mixed dried herbs

2 tbsp olive oil

salt and pepper

1 To make the dough, mix the yeast and sugar with 4 tablespoons of the water in a bowl. Leave in a warm place for 15 minutes or until frothy.

2 In a separate bowl, mix the flour with the salt and make a well in the centre. Add the oil, yeast mixture and remaining water. Mix into a smooth dough using a wooden spoon.

3 Turn the dough out on to a floured work surface and knead for 4–5 minutes, or until smooth. Return the dough to the mixing bowl, cover with an oiled sheet of clingfilm and leave in a warm place to rise for 30 minutes, or until the dough has doubled in size.

4 Knead the dough for 2 minutes, then divide it into 8 balls. Roll out each portion thinly to form a round about 10 cm/4 inches wide, then place the 8 dough rounds on an oiled baking tray and push out the edges until even. The dough should be no more than 5 mm/¼ inch thick because it will rise during cooking.

5 To make the topping, grate the courgettes finely. Cover them with absorbent kitchen paper and leave to stand for about 10 minutes to soak up some of the juices.

6 Spread 2–3 teaspoons of the passata over each pizza base and top with the grated courgettes, pancetta and olives. Season with pepper and add a sprinkling of mixed dried herbs to taste, then drizzle with olive oil.

7 Bake in a preheated oven, 200°C/400°F/Gas Mark 6, for 15 minutes, or until crispy. Season to taste and serve hot.

creamy ham pizzas

serves four

250 g/9 oz flaky pastry, well chilled

3 tbsp butter

1 red onion, chopped

1 garlic clove, chopped

5 tbsp plain white flour

300 ml/10 fl oz milk

50 g/1¾ oz finely grated Parmesan cheese, plus extra for sprinkling

2 eggs, hard-boiled and cut into quarters

100 g/3½ oz Italian pork sausage, such as feline salame, cut into strips

salt and pepper

fresh thyme sprigs, to garnish

1 Fold the pastry in half and grate it into 4 individual flan tins measuring 10 cm/4 inches across. Using a floured fork, press the pastry flakes down evenly, making sure that there are no holes and that the pastry comes up the sides of the tins.

2 Line with foil and bake blind in a preheated oven, 220°C/425°F/Gas Mark 7, for 10 minutes. Reduce the heat to 200°C/400°F/Gas Mark 6, remove the foil and cook for 15 minutes, or until golden and set.

3 Heat the butter in a saucepan. Add the onion and garlic and cook for 5–6 minutes, or until softened.

4 Add the flour, stirring well to coat the onion. Gradually stir in the milk to make a thick sauce.

5 Season the sauce with salt and pepper to taste, then stir in the Parmesan cheese. Do not reheat once the cheese has been added or the sauce will become too stringy.

6 Spread the sauce over the cooked pastry cases. Decorate with the eggs and strips of sausage.

7 Sprinkle with a little extra Parmesan cheese, return to the oven and bake for 5 minutes, just to heat through.

8 Serve immediately, garnished with sprigs of fresh thyme.

gnocchi romana

serves four

700 ml/1¼ pints milk
pinch of freshly grated nutmeg
6 tbsp butter, plus extra for greasing
225 g/8 oz semolina
125 g/4½ oz freshly grated
   Parmesan cheese
2 eggs, beaten
55 g/2 oz Gruyère cheese, grated
salt and pepper
fresh basil sprigs, to garnish

1 Pour the milk into a large saucepan and bring to the boil. Remove the pan from the heat and stir in the nutmeg, 2 tablespoons of the butter and salt and pepper to taste.

2 Gradually stir the semolina into the milk, whisking to prevent lumps from forming, then return to the hob over a low heat. Simmer, stirring constantly, for about 10 minutes, or until very thick.

3 Beat 55 g/2 oz of the grated Parmesan cheese into the semolina mixture, then beat in the eggs. Continue beating the mixture until smooth. Leave the mixture to cool slightly.

4 Spread out the cooled semolina mixture in an even layer on a sheet of baking paper, smoothing the surface with a damp palette knife until it is 1 cm/½ inch thick. Leave to cool completely, then chill in the refrigerator for 1 hour.

5 Remove the chilled mixture from the refrigerator. Stamp out rounds of gnocchi about 4 cm/1½ inches wide using a plain, greased pastry cutter.

6 Grease a shallow ovenproof dish or 4 individual ovenproof dishes. Arrange the gnocchi trimmings over the base of the dish or dishes and then cover them with the rounds of gnocchi, overlapping them slightly.

7 Melt the remaining butter and drizzle it over the gnocchi. Sprinkle over the remaining Parmesan cheese, then sprinkle the Gruyère cheese evenly over the top of the dish.

8 Bake in a preheated oven, 200°C/400°F/Gas Mark 6, for 25–30 minutes, until the top is crisp and golden. Serve hot garnished with fresh basil sprigs.

spinach & ricotta shells

serves four

400 g/14 oz dried lumache rigate
   grande pasta
5 tbsp olive oil
55 g/2 oz fresh white breadcrumbs
125 ml/4 fl oz milk
300 g/10½ oz frozen spinach,
   thawed and drained
225 g/8 oz ricotta cheese
pinch of freshly grated nutmeg
400 g/14 oz canned chopped
   tomatoes, drained
1 garlic clove, crushed
salt and pepper

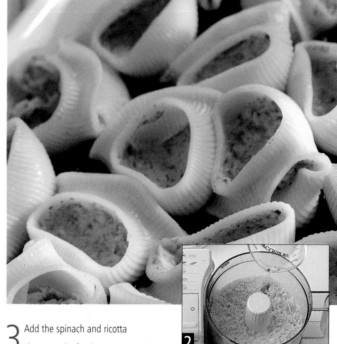

1 Bring a large saucepan of lightly salted water to the boil. Add the pasta and 1 tablespoon of the olive oil, bring back to the boil and cook for 8–10 minutes, until just tender but still firm to the bite. Drain the pasta, refresh under cold running water, drain again and set aside until required.

2 Put the breadcrumbs, milk and 3 tablespoons of the remaining olive oil into a food processor and process until blended.

3 Add the spinach and ricotta cheese to the food processor and process to a smooth mixture. Transfer to a bowl, stir in the nutmeg and season with salt and pepper to taste.

4 Mix the tomatoes, garlic and remaining oil together in a bowl and spoon the mixture into the base of a large ovenproof dish.

5 Carefully fill the lumache with the spinach and ricotta mixture using a teaspoon, then arrange the filled

pasta shapes on top of the tomato mixture in the dish. Cover and bake in a preheated oven, 180°C/350°F/Gas Mark 4, for 20 minutes. Serve the lumache hot, straight from the dish.

tricolour timballini

serves four

1 tbsp butter, for greasing

55 g/2 oz dried white breadcrumbs

175 g/6 oz dried tricolour spaghetti,
   broken into 5-cm/2-inch lengths

3 tbsp olive oil

1 egg yolk

125 g/4½ oz Gruyère cheese, grated

300 ml/10 fl oz Béchamel Sauce
   (see page 206)

1 onion, chopped finely

1 bay leaf

150 ml/5 fl oz dry white wine

150 ml/5 fl oz passata

1 tbsp tomato purée

salt and pepper

fresh basil leaves, to garnish

1 Grease 4 x 175-ml/6-fl-oz cup moulds or ramekins with the butter. Evenly coat the insides with half of the breadcrumbs.

2 Bring a saucepan of lightly salted water to the boil. Add the spaghetti and 1 tablespoon of oil and cook for 8–10 minutes, or until just tender but firm to the bite. Drain and transfer to a mixing bowl. Add the egg yolk and cheese to the pasta and season with salt and pepper.

3 Pour the béchamel sauce into the bowl containing the pasta and mix. Spoon the mixture into the ramekins and sprinkle over the remaining breadcrumbs.

4 Stand the ramekins on a baking tray and bake in a preheated oven, 220°C/425°F/Gas Mark 7, for 20 minutes. Remove from the oven and leave to stand for 10 minutes.

5 Meanwhile, heat the remaining olive oil in a large saucepan, add the chopped onion and bay leaf and cook over a low heat for 2–3 minutes.

6 Stir in the white wine, passata and tomato purée and season with salt and pepper to taste. Simmer gently for 20 minutes, until thickened. Remove and discard the bay leaf.

7 Turn the timballini out on to serving plates, garnish with basil and serve with the tomato sauce.

three cheese bake

serves four

1 tbsp butter, for greasing

400 g/14 oz dried penne pasta

1 tbsp olive oil

2 eggs, beaten

350 g/12 oz ricotta cheese

25 g/1 oz fresh basil leaves, plus
extra to garnish

100 g/3½ oz mozzarella or halloumi
cheese, grated

70 g/2½ oz freshly grated
Parmesan cheese

salt and pepper

VARIATION

Try substituting smoked Bavarian
cheese for the mozzarella or
halloumi and grated Cheddar
cheese for the Parmesan, for a
slightly different, but just as
delicious flavour.

1 Lightly grease a large ovenproof
dish with the butter.

2 Bring a large saucepan of lightly
salted water to the boil. Add the
penne and olive oil and cook for
8–10 minutes, until just tender but still
firm to the bite. Drain the pasta, set
aside and keep warm.

3 Beat the eggs into the ricotta
cheese and season to taste.

4 Spoon half of the penne into the
base of the prepared dish and
cover with half of the basil leaves.

5 Spoon over half of the ricotta
cheese mixture. Sprinkle over
the mozzarella or halloumi cheese,
then top with the remaining basil
leaves. Cover with the remaining
penne, then spoon over the remaining
ricotta cheese mixture. Lightly sprinkle
the freshly grated Parmesan cheese
over the top.

6 Bake in a preheated oven,
190°C/375°F/Gas Mark 5, for
30–40 minutes, until golden brown
and the cheese topping is bubbling.
Garnish with fresh basil leaves and
serve the bake immediately.

macaroni bake

serves four

450 g/1 lb dried short-cut macaroni

1 tbsp olive oil

4 tbsp beef dripping

450 g/1 lb potatoes, thinly sliced

450 g/1 lb onions, sliced

225 g/8 oz mozzarella
   cheese, grated

150 ml/5 fl oz double cream

salt and pepper

crusty brown bread and butter,
   to serve

VARIATION

For a stronger flavour, use
mozzarella affumicata, a
smoked version of this cheese,
or Gruyère cheese, instead
of the mozzarella.

1 Bring a large saucepan of lightly salted water to the boil. Add the macaroni and oil, bring back to the boil and cook for about 12 minutes, or until the pasta is just tender but still firm to the bite. Drain thoroughly and set aside.

2 Melt the beef dripping in a large flameproof casserole over a low heat, then remove from the heat.

3 Make alternate layers of potatoes, onions, macaroni and grated mozzarella cheese in the casserole, seasoning well with salt and pepper between each layer and finishing with a layer of cheese on top. Finally, pour the cream over the top layer of cheese.

4 Bake in a preheated oven, 200°C/ 400°F/Gas Mark 6, for 25 minutes. Remove the casserole from the oven and carefully brown the top of the bake under a hot grill.

5 Serve the bake straight from the casserole with crusty brown bread and butter as a main course. Alternatively, serve as a vegetable accompaniment to a main course.

pancetta & pecorino cakes

serves four

2 tbsp butter, plus extra for greasing

100 g/3 ½ oz pancetta,
   rind removed

225 g/8 oz self-raising flour

75 g/2¾ oz pecorino cheese, grated

150 ml/5 fl oz milk, plus extra
   for glazing

1 tbsp tomato ketchup

1 tsp Worcestershire sauce

400 g/14 oz dried farfalle pasta

1 tbsp olive oil

salt

TO SERVE

3 tbsp Pesto Sauce (see page 7),
   or anchovy sauce (optional)

green salad

1 Grease a baking tray with a little butter. Place the pancetta under a preheated hot grill until cooked, allow to cool, then chop finely.

2 Sieve the flour and a pinch of salt into a mixing bowl, then rub in the butter with your fingertips until the mixture resembles breadcrumbs. Add the chopped pancetta and one-third of the grated cheese to the mixture and stir to blend.

3 In a separate bowl, mix together the milk, tomato ketchup and Worcestershire sauce and add to the dry ingredients. Bring together with your fingers to form a soft dough.

4 Roll out the dough on a lightly floured work surface into an 18-cm/7-inch round. Brush with a little milk to glaze and cut into 8 wedges.

5 Arrange the dough wedges on the prepared baking tray and sprinkle over the remaining grated cheese. Bake in a preheated oven, 200°C/400°F/ Gas Mark 6, for 20 minutes.

6 Meanwhile, bring a saucepan of lightly salted water to the boil. Add the farfalle and the oil and cook for 8–10 minutes, until just tender but still firm to the bite. Drain and transfer to a large serving dish. Top with the cooked pancetta and pecorino cakes. Serve with the sauce of your choice and a green salad.

garlic & pine kernel tarts

serves four

4 slices wholemeal or granary bread

50 g/1¾ oz pine kernels

150 g/5½ oz butter

5 garlic cloves, halved

2 tbsp fresh oregano, chopped,
    plus extra for garnish

4 stoned black olives, halved

fresh oregano leaves, to garnish

VARIATION

Puff pastry can be used for the tarts. Use 200 g/7 oz puff pastry to line 4 tartlet tins. Chill in the refrigerator for 20 minutes. Line the pastry with foil and bake blind for 10 minutes. Remove the foil and bake for 3–4 minutes, or until the pastry is set. Leave to cool, then continue from step 2, adding 2 tablespoons breadcrumbs to the mixture instead of the bread offcuts.

---

1 Flatten the bread slightly with a rolling pin. Cut out 4 rounds of bread about 10 cm/4 inches wide using a pastry cutter, to fit 4 individual tartlet tins. Use them to line the tins. Reserve the offcuts of bread and chill them in the refrigerator for 10 minutes, or until required.

2 Meanwhile, place the pine kernels on a baking tray and toast them under a preheated grill for 2–3 minutes, or until golden.

3 Put the bread offcuts, toasted pine kernels, butter, garlic and oregano into a food processor and process for about 20 seconds. Alternatively, pound the ingredients by hand with a mortar and pestle. The mixture should have a coarse texture.

4 Spoon the mixture into the bread-lined tins and top with the olives. Bake in a preheated oven, 200°C/ 400°F/Gas Mark 6, for 10–15 minutes, or until golden.

5 Transfer the tarts to serving plates and serve warm, garnished with fresh oregano leaves.

provençal tart

1 Roll out the pastry on a lightly floured work surface and use it to line a 20-cm/8-inch loose-bottomed quiche or flan tin. Chill in the refrigerator for 20 minutes.

2 Meanwhile, heat 2 tablespoons of the olive oil in a frying pan. Add the red and green peppers and cook over a low heat for 8 minutes, until softened, stirring frequently.

3 Whisk the double cream and egg together in a bowl and season to taste with salt and pepper. Stir in the cooked peppers.

4 Heat the remaining oil in a separate frying pan and cook the courgette slices over a medium heat, stirring frequently, for 4–5 minutes, until lightly browned.

5 Pour the egg and pepper mixture into the pastry case.

6 Arrange the courgette slices around the edge of the tart.

7 Bake the tart in a preheated oven, 180°C/ 350°F/Gas Mark 4, for 35–40 minutes, or until just set and golden. Serve hot or cold.

fresh tomato tarts

serves six

plain flour, for dusting

250 g/9 oz ready-made puff pastry,
   thawed if frozen

1 egg, beaten

2 tbsp Pesto Sauce (see page 7)

6 plum tomatoes, sliced

salt and pepper

fresh thyme leaves,
   to garnish (optional)

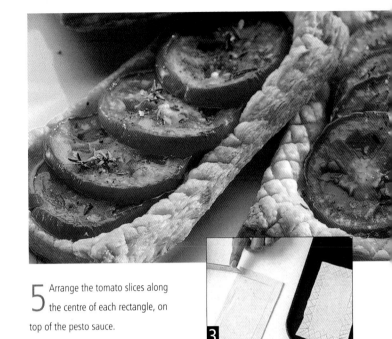

1 On a lightly floured work surface, roll out the pastry into a rectangle measuring 30 x 25 cm/12 x 10 inches.

2 Cut the rectangle in half and divide each half into 3 pieces to make 6 even-sized rectangles. Chill in the refrigerator for 20 minutes.

3 Lightly score the edges of the pastry rectangles and brush them with the beaten egg.

4 Spread the pesto sauce over the rectangles, dividing it equally between them, leaving 2½-cm/1-inch borders around the edges.

5 Arrange the tomato slices along the centre of each rectangle, on top of the pesto sauce.

6 Season well with salt and pepper to taste and lightly sprinkle with fresh thyme leaves, if you wish.

7 Bake in a preheated oven, 200°C/400°F/Gas Mark 6, for 15–20 minutes, until well risen and golden brown.

8 Transfer the tomato tarts to warmed serving plates straight from the oven and serve while they are still piping hot.

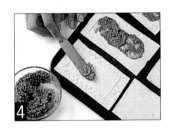

3

4

5

vegetable pasta nests

serves four

175 g/6 oz dried spaghetti

1 aubergine, halved lengthways
and sliced

1 courgette, diced

1 red pepper, deseeded and
chopped diagonally

6 tbsp olive oil

2 garlic cloves, crushed

4 tbsp butter or margarine, melted,
plus extra for greasing

15 g/½ oz dried white breadcrumbs

salt and pepper

fresh parsley sprigs, to garnish

COOK'S TIP

The Italian term *al dente* means
'to the bite' and describes
cooked pasta that is not too soft
and still has a firmness to it. Start
timing the pasta from the
moment the water comes back to
the boil. Begin testing, by biting
a small piece of pasta between
your front teeth, about 2 minutes
before the specified cooking time
is up. Drain as soon as it is ready,
or it will become soggy.

1 Bring a saucepan of lightly salted water to the boil, add the spaghetti, bring back to the boil and cook for 8–10 minutes, until tender but still firm to the bite. Drain and set aside.

2 Place the aubergine, courgette and pepper on a baking tray.

3 Mix the oil and garlic together and pour over the vegetables, tossing to coat well.

4 Cook under a preheated hot grill for about 10 minutes, turning occasionally, until tender and lightly charred. Set aside and keep warm.

5 Lightly grease 4 Yorkshire pudding tins and divide the spaghetti between them. Curl the spaghetti to form nests using 2 forks.

6 Brush the pasta nests with melted butter or margarine and sprinkle with the breadcrumbs. Bake in a preheated oven, 200°C/400°F/Gas Mark 6, for 15 minutes, or until lightly golden. Remove the pasta nests from the tins and transfer to serving plates. Divide the grilled vegetables between the pasta nests, season to taste with salt and pepper and garnish with fresh parsley sprigs.

mini cheese & onion tarts

makes twelve

PASTRY

100 g/3½ oz plain flour, plus extra
for dusting

¼ tsp salt

5½ tbsp butter, diced

1–2 tbsp water

FILLING

1 egg, beaten

100 ml/3½ fl oz single cream

50 g/1¾ oz Red Leicester
cheese, grated

3 spring onions, chopped finely

salt

cayenne pepper

1 To make the pastry, sieve the flour and salt into a mixing bowl. Rub in the butter with your fingertips until the mixture resembles breadcrumbs. Stir in the water, bring together to form a dough and shape the dough into a ball. Cover with clingfilm and leave to chill in the refrigerator for 30 minutes.

2 Roll out the dough on a lightly floured work surface. Stamp out 12 rounds from the pastry using a 7.5-cm/3-inch biscuit cutter, and use them to line a tartlet tin.

3 To make the filling, whisk the beaten egg, cream, Red Leicester cheese and spring onions together in a jug. Season to taste with salt and cayenne pepper.

4 Pour the filling into the pastry cases and bake in a preheated oven, 180°C/350°F/Gas Mark 4, for about 20–25 minutes, or until the filling is just set and the pastry is golden brown. Transfer the tartlets to a warmed serving platter if serving warm, or to a wire rack to cool if serving cold.

ham & cheese lattice pies

makes six

1 tbsp butter, for greasing

250 g/9 oz ready-made puff pastry,
    thawed if frozen

plain flour, for dusting

50 g/1¾ oz ham, chopped finely

125 g/4½ oz full-fat soft cheese

2 tbsp snipped fresh chives

1 egg, beaten

35 g/1¼ oz freshly grated
    Parmesan cheese

pepper

1 Grease 2 baking trays with the butter. Roll out the pastry thinly on a lightly floured work surface. Cut out 12 rectangles, each measuring 15 x 5 cm/6 x 2 inches.

2 Place the rectangles on the baking trays and chill in the refrigerator for 30 minutes.

3 Meanwhile, combine the ham, soft cheese and chives in a small bowl. Season with pepper to taste.

4 Spread the ham and cheese mixture along the centre of 6 of the rectangles, leaving a 2.5-cm/1-inch border around the edges. Brush the borders with the beaten egg.

5 To make the lattice pattern, fold the remaining rectangles lengthways. Leaving a 2.5-cm/1-inch border, cut vertical lines across the folded edge of the pastry rectangles.

6 Unfold the latticed rectangles and place them over the rectangles topped with the ham and cheese mixture. Press the edges well to seal them and lightly sprinkle the pies with the Parmesan cheese.

7 Bake in a preheated oven, 180°C/350°F/Gas Mark 4. for 15–20 minutes. Serve hot, or transfer to a wire rack to cool and serve cold.

pissaladière

serves eight

1 tbsp butter, for greasing

4 tbsp olive oil

700 g/1 lb 9 oz red onions,
   sliced thinly

2 garlic cloves, crushed

2 tsp caster sugar

2 tbsp red wine vinegar

salt and pepper

plain flour, for dusting

350 g/12 oz ready-made puff
   pastry, thawed if frozen

TOPPING

100 g/3½ oz canned anchovy fillets

12 stoned green olives

1 tsp dried marjoram

VARIATION

Cut the pissaladière into squares
or triangles for easy finger food
at a party or barbecue.

---

1 Lightly grease a Swiss roll tin with butter. Heat the oil in a large, heavy-based saucepan. Add the onions and garlic and cook over a low heat for about 30 minutes, stirring occasionally.

2 Add the sugar and red wine vinegar to the saucepan and season with plenty of salt and pepper.

3 On a lightly floured surface, roll out the pastry to a rectangle measuring 33 x 23 cm/13 x 9 inches. Place the pastry rectangle in the prepared tin, pushing the pastry well into the corners of the tin.

4 Spread the onion mixture evenly over the pastry.

5 To make the decorative topping, arrange the anchovy fillets in a criss-cross pattern on top of the onion mixture, place the green olives in between the anchovies, then sprinkle the marjoram over the top.

6 Bake in a preheated oven, 220°C/425°F/Gas Mark 7, for 20–25 minutes, until the pissaladière is lightly golden. Serve piping hot, straight from the oven.

tuna-stuffed tomatoes

serves four

4 plum tomatoes

2 tbsp sun-dried tomato paste

2 egg yolks

2 tsp lemon juice

finely grated rind of 1 lemon

4 tbsp olive oil

115g/4 oz canned tuna, drained

2 tbsp capers, rinsed

salt and pepper

TO GARNISH

2 sun-dried tomatoes in oil, drained
and cut into strips

fresh basil leaves

1 Halve the tomatoes and scoop out the seeds. Divide the sun-dried tomato paste between the tomato halves and spread around the inside of the skins.

2 Place the tomatoes on a baking tray and roast in a preheated oven, 200°C/400°F/Gas Mark 6, for 12–15 minutes. Leave to cool slightly.

3 Meanwhile, to make the mayonnaise, put the egg yolks, lemon juice and lemon rind into a food processor and process until smooth.

Once mixed, and with the motor still running, gradually add the olive oil. Stop the food processor as soon as the mayonnaise has thickened. Alternatively, use a hand whisk to beat the mixture until it thickens.

4 Add the tuna and capers to the mayonnaise, season and stir.

5 Spoon the mayonnaise mixture into the tomatoes and garnish with sun-dried tomato strips and basil. Return to the oven for a few minutes to warm through, or serve chilled.

baked tuna & ricotta rigatoni

serves four

1 tbsp butter, for greasing

450 g/1 lb dried rigatoni pasta

1 tbsp olive oil

200 g/7 oz canned flaked
    tuna, drained

225 g/8 oz ricotta cheese

125 ml/4 fl oz double cream

225 g/8 oz freshly grated
    Parmesan cheese

125 g/4½ oz sun-dried tomatoes in
    oil, drained and sliced

salt and pepper

VARIATION

For a vegetarian alternative to
this recipe, simply substitute a
mixture of stoned and chopped
black olives and chopped
walnuts for the tuna.

1 Lightly grease a large ovenproof
dish with the butter.

2 Bring a large saucepan of lightly
salted water to the boil. Add the
rigatoni and olive oil, bring back to the
boil and cook for 8–10 minutes, until
just tender but still firm to the bite.
Drain the pasta, rinse in cold water and
set aside until cool enough to handle.

3 Meanwhile, mix the flaked tuna
and ricotta cheese together in a
bowl until thoroughly blended into a
soft paste. Spoon the mixture into a
piping bag and use it to fill the
rigatoni. Arrange the filled pasta tubes
side by side in a single layer in the
prepared ovenproof dish.

4 Mix the cream and grated
Parmesan cheese and season
with salt and pepper to taste.

5 Spoon the cream mixture over
the rigatoni and top with the
sun-dried tomatoes, arranged in a
criss-cross pattern. Bake in a preheated
oven, 200°C/400°F/Gas Mark 6, for
20 minutes. Serve immediately, straight
from the dish.

roasted seafood

serves four

600 g/1 lb 5 oz new potatoes

3 red onions, cut into wedges

2 courgettes, cut into chunks

8 garlic cloves

2 lemons, cut into wedges

4 fresh rosemary sprigs

4 tbsp olive oil

350 g/12 oz unpeeled prawns, preferably raw

2 small prepared squid, chopped into rings

4 tomatoes, quartered

VARIATION

Most vegetables are suitable for roasting in the oven. Try adding 450 g/1 lb pumpkin, squash or aubergine, if you prefer.

1 Scrub the potatoes to remove any dirt. Cut any large potatoes in half. Place the potatoes in a large roasting tin, together with the onions, courgettes, garlic, lemon wedges and rosemary sprigs.

2 Pour the oil into the roasting tin and toss to coat the vegetables. Cook in a preheated oven, 200°C/400°F/Gas Mark 6, for 40 minutes, turning occasionally, until the potatoes are cooked and tender.

3 Once the potatoes are tender, add the prawns, squid rings and tomato quarters, tossing gently to coat in the hot oil, and roast for 10 minutes. All of the vegetables should be cooked through and slightly charred for full flavour, and all the prawns should have turned pink.

4 Transfer the roasted seafood and vegetables to warmed serving plates using a slotted spoon, and serve immediately.

Savoury Meals

This chapter presents a mouthwatering array of savoury dishes to tempt any palate, including pies, pastries, tarts and flans, as well as a variety of delicious savoury bakes. The choice is wide, including Cheese Pudding, Red Onion Tart Tatin and Asparagus & Cheese Tart. Fish fans can choose from a wide menu, including Smoky Fish Pie, Fresh Baked Sardines, and Fillets of Red Mullet & Pasta. Meat and poultry dishes include Red Roast Pork in Soy Sauce, Fruity Lamb Casserole and Italian Chicken Parcels.

vermicelli & vegetable flan

serves four

6 tbsp butter, plus extra for greasing

225 g/8 oz dried vermicelli
  or spaghetti

1 tbsp olive oil

1 onion, chopped

140 g/5 oz button mushrooms

1 green pepper, deseeded and
  sliced into thin rings

150 ml/5 fl oz milk

3 eggs, lightly beaten

2 tbsp double cream

1 tsp dried oregano

freshly grated nutmeg

15 g/½ oz freshly grated
  Parmesan cheese

salt and pepper

tomato and basil salad,
  to serve (optional)

1 Generously grease a 20-cm/ 8-inch loose-bottomed flan tin with a little butter.

2 Bring a large saucepan of lightly salted water to the boil. Add the vermicelli or spaghetti and olive oil, bring back to the boil and cook for 8–10 minutes, until tender but still firm to the bite. Drain, return to the saucepan, add 2 tablespoons of the butter and shake the saucepan to coat the pasta.

3 Press the pasta on to the base and around the sides of the flan tin to make a flan case.

4 Melt the remaining butter in a large frying pan over a medium heat. Add the chopped onion and cook over a low heat, stirring occasionally, until translucent.

5 Add the mushrooms and pepper rings to the frying pan and cook, stirring, for 2–3 minutes. Spoon the onion, mushroom and pepper mixture into the flan case and press it evenly into the base.

6 Beat together the milk, eggs and cream, stir in the oregano and season to taste with nutmeg and pepper. Carefully pour the mixture over the vegetables, then sprinkle with the Parmesan cheese.

7 Bake the flan in a preheated oven, 180°C/350°F/Gas Mark 4, for about 40–45 minutes, or until the filling has set.

8 Carefully slide the flan out of the tin and serve warm with a tomato and basil salad, if you wish.

asparagus & cheese tart

serves six

250 g/9 oz ready-made shortcrust
   pastry, thawed

plain flour, for dusting
   if frozen

250 g/9 oz asparagus

1 tbsp vegetable oil

1 red onion, chopped finely

25 g/1 oz hazelnuts, chopped

200 g/7 oz goat's cheese

2 eggs, beaten

4 tbsp single cream

salt and pepper

1 Roll out the pastry on a lightly floured work surface and use it to line a 24-cm/9½-inch loose-bottomed quiche or flan tin. Prick the base of the pastry with a fork and chill in the refrigerator for 30 minutes.

2 Line the pastry case with foil and baking beans and bake in a preheated oven, 190°C/375°F/Gas Mark 5, for 15 minutes.

3 Remove the foil and beans and bake for a further 15 minutes.

4 Cook the asparagus in boiling water for 2–3 minutes, drain, and cut into bite-sized pieces.

5 Heat the oil in a small frying pan and cook the onion over a low heat, stirring occasionally, until soft and lightly golden. Spoon the asparagus, onion and hazelnuts into the prepared pastry case.

6 Beat the cheese, eggs and cream together in a bowl until smooth, or place in a food processor and process until smooth. Season well with salt and pepper, then pour over the mixture in the pastry case.

7 Bake in the preheated oven for 15–20 minutes, or until the filling is just set. Serve warm or cold.

VARIATION

Omit the hazelnuts and sprinkle grated Parmesan cheese over the top of the tart just before cooking, if you wish.

cheese pudding

serves four

1 tbsp butter, for greasing

150 g/5½ oz fresh white
   breadcrumbs

100 g/3½ oz Gruyère cheese, grated

150 ml/5 fl oz hand-hot milk

125 g/4½ oz butter, melted

2 eggs, separated

2 tbsp chopped fresh parsley

salt and pepper

green salad, to serve

1 Grease a 1-litre/1¾-pint ovenproof dish with the butter.

2 Place the breadcrumbs and cheese in a bowl and mix. Pour the milk over the cheese and breadcrumb mixture and stir to blend. Add the melted butter, egg yolks, parsley and salt and pepper to taste, and mix well.

3 In a separate bowl, whisk the egg whites until firm, but not stiff. Gently fold in the cheese mixture in a figure-of-eight movement.

4 Transfer the mixture to the prepared ovenproof dish and gently smooth the surface with a palette knife.

5 Bake the pudding in a preheated oven, 190°C/375°F/Gas Mark 5, for about 45 minutes, or until golden and slightly risen, and a fine metal skewer inserted into the centre of the pudding comes out clean.

6 Serve the cheese pudding hot, with a green salad.

2

3

3

red onion tart tatin

serves four

4 tbsp butter

6 tsp sugar

500 g/1 lb 2 oz red
onions, quartered

3 tbsp red wine vinegar

2 tbsp fresh thyme leaves

plain flour, for dusting

250 g/9 oz ready-made puff pastry,
thawed if frozen

salt and pepper

VARIATION

Replace the red onions with
shallots, leaving them whole,
if you wish.

COOK'S TIP

A heavy, cast iron frying pan is
best for making this classic
upside down tart, as it
distributes the heat evenly so
that the onions will not stick.

1 Place the butter and sugar in a
23-cm/9-inch ovenproof frying
pan and cook over a medium heat until
melted and blended.

2 Add the red onion quarters and
sweat over a low heat, stirring
occasionally, for 10–15 minutes, until
golden and caramelized.

3 Add the red wine vinegar and
thyme leaves to the pan. Season
with salt and pepper to taste, then
simmer over a medium heat until the
liquid has reduced and the red onion
pieces are coated in the buttery sauce.

4 On a lightly floured work surface,
roll out the pastry into a round
slightly larger than the frying pan.

5 Place the pastry over the onion
mixture in the pan and press
down, tucking in the edges to seal it.

6 Bake in a preheated oven,
180°C/350°F/Gas Mark 4, for
20–25 minutes, until the pastry is firm
and golden brown. Remove the tart
from the oven and leave to stand for
10 minutes.

7 To turn out, place a serving plate
over the frying pan and, holding
them firmly together, carefully invert so
that the pastry becomes the base of
the tart. Serve the tart warm.

celery & onion pies

makes twelve

PASTRY

125 g/4½ oz plain flour, plus extra
for dusting

½ tsp salt

2 tbsp butter, diced

25 g/1 oz mature cheese, grated

3–4 tbsp cold water

FILLING

4 tbsp butter

125 g/4½ oz celery, chopped finely

2 garlic cloves, crushed

1 small onion, chopped finely

1 tbsp plain flour

50 ml/2 fl oz milk

salt

pinch of cayenne pepper

1 To make the filling, melt the butter in a frying pan. Add the celery, garlic and onion and cook over a medium heat, stirring occasionally, for about 5 minutes, or until softened.

2 Reduce the heat and stir in the flour, then the milk. Bring back to a simmer, then cook gently over a low heat until the mixture is thick, stirring frequently. Season to taste with salt and cayenne pepper. Leave to cool.

3 To make the pastry, sieve the flour and salt into a mixing bowl and rub in the butter with your fingertips. Stir in the cheese and the cold water and bring together to form a dough.

4 Roll out three-quarters of the dough on a lightly floured work surface. Stamp out 12 rounds using a 6-cm/2½-inch fluted biscuit cutter. Line a tartlet tin with the rounds.

5 Divide the filling between the pastry cases. Roll out the remaining dough and stamp out 12 rounds using a 5-cm/2-inch cutter, Place the smaller rounds on top of the pie filling and press to seal. Make a slit in each pie and chill in the refrigerator for 30 minutes.

6 Bake in a preheated oven, 220°C/425°F/Gas Mark 7, for 15–20 minutes. Leave to cool in the tin for 10 minutes before turning out. Serve warm.

onion tart

250 g/9 oz ready-made shortcrust
  pastry, thawed if frozen

plain flour, for dusting

3 tbsp butter

75 g/2¾ oz bacon, chopped

700 g/1 lb 9 oz onions, sliced thinly

2 eggs, beaten

50 g/1¾ oz freshly grated
  Parmesan cheese

1 tsp dried sage

salt and pepper

VARIATION

To make a vegetarian version
of this tart, replace the bacon
with the same amount of
chopped mushrooms.

---

1 Roll out the pastry on a lightly
  floured work surface and use it to
line a 24-cm/9½-inch loose-bottomed
quiche or flan tin.

2 Prick the base of the pastry with a
  fork and chill in the refrigerator for
30 minutes.

3 Meanwhile, heat the butter in
  a saucepan, add the bacon and
onions and sweat over a low heat for
about 25 minutes, or until tender. If
the onion slices start to brown, add
1 tablespoon of water to the saucepan.

4 Add the beaten eggs to the onion
  mixture and stir in the Parmesan
cheese and sage. Season with salt and
pepper to taste.

5 Spoon the mixture into the
  prepared pastry case.

6 Bake in a preheated oven,
  180°C/350°F/Gas Mark 4, for
20–30 minutes, or until the onion
filling has just set and the pastry is
crisp and golden.

7 Leave in the tin to cool slightly.
  Serve warm or cold.

gorgonzola & pumpkin pizza

serves four

PIZZA DOUGH

10 g/¼ oz easy-blend dried yeast

1 tsp sugar

250 ml/9 fl oz hand-hot water

175 g/6 oz plain wholemeal flour

175 g/6 oz strong plain white

    flour, plus extra for dusting

1 tsp salt

1 tbsp olive oil, for brushing

1 fresh rosemary sprig, to garnish

TOPPING

400 g/14 oz pumpkin or squash,

    peeled and cubed

1 tbsp olive oil

1 pear, cored, peeled and sliced

100 g/3½ oz Gorgonzola cheese

1 Place the yeast and sugar in a measuring jug and mix with 4 tablespoons of the water. Leave the yeast mixture in a warm place for about 15 minutes, or until frothy.

2 Mix both of the flours with the salt and make a well in the centre. Add the oil, yeast mixture and remaining water. Bring together using a wooden spoon to form a dough.

3 Turn the dough out on to a floured work surface and knead for 4–5 minutes, or until smooth.

4 Return the dough to the bowl and cover with an oiled sheet of clingfilm. Leave to rise for 30 minutes, or until doubled in size.

5 Brush a baking tray with oil. Knead the dough for 2 minutes to knock it back. Roll out into a long oval shape, then place on the prepared baking tray and push out the edges until even. The dough should be no more than 5 mm/¼ inch thick because it will rise during cooking.

6 To make the topping, place the pumpkin in a shallow roasting tin. Drizzle with the oil and cook under a preheated medium grill for 20 minutes, or until soft and lightly golden.

7 Arrange the pear and pumpkin on top of the dough and brush with the oil from the roasting tin. Crumble over the Gorgonzola. Bake in a preheated oven, 200°C/400°F/Gas Mark 6, for 15 minutes, or until the base is golden. Garnish with rosemary.

stuffed aubergines

serves four

225 g/8 oz dried penne pasta

4 tbsp olive oil, plus extra
   for brushing

2 aubergines

1 large onion, chopped

2 garlic cloves, crushed

400 g/14 oz canned
   chopped tomatoes

2 tsp dried oregano

55 g/2 oz mozzarella cheese,
   sliced thinly

25 g/1 oz freshly grated
   Parmesan cheese

25 g/1 oz dried white or
   wholemeal breadcrumbs

salt and pepper

salad leaves, to serve

1 Bring a large saucepan of lightly salted water to the boil. Add the pasta and 1 tablespoon of the olive oil, bring back to the boil and cook for 8–10 minutes, or until just tender but still firm to the bite. Drain, return to the saucepan, cover and keep warm.

2 Cut the aubergines in half lengthways and score around the inside with a sharp knife, being careful not to pierce the shells. Scoop out the flesh with a spoon. Brush the insides of the shells with olive oil. Chop the flesh and set aside.

3 Heat the remaining oil in a frying pan. Cook the onion until translucent. Add the garlic and cook for 1 minute. Add the aubergine flesh and cook, stirring frequently, for 5 minutes. Add the tomatoes and oregano and season to taste with salt and pepper. Bring to the boil and simmer for 10 minutes, or until thickened. Remove the frying pan from the heat and stir in the pasta.

4 Brush a baking tray with oil and arrange the aubergine shells on the tray in a single layer. Divide half of

the tomato and pasta mixture between them. Scatter over the slices of mozzarella, then pile the remaining tomato and pasta mixture on top. Mix the Parmesan cheese and breadcrumbs in a small bowl and sprinkle over the top, patting it lightly into the mixture.

5 Bake in a preheated oven, 200°C/400°F/Gas Mark 6, for about 25 minutes, or until the topping is golden brown. Serve hot with a selection of mixed salad leaves.

smoky fish pie

serves four

900 g/2 lb smoked haddock or
    cod fillets

600 ml/1 pint skimmed milk

2 bay leaves

115 g/4 oz button mushrooms, cut
    into quarters

115 g/4 oz frozen peas

115 g/4 oz frozen sweetcorn kernels

675 g/1½ lb potatoes, diced

5 tbsp low-fat natural yogurt

4 tbsp chopped fresh parsley

55 g/2 oz smoked salmon, sliced
    into thin strips

3 tbsp cornflour

25 g/1 oz smoked cheese, grated

salt and pepper

1 Place the fish in a saucepan and add the milk and bay leaves. Bring to the boil, cover and simmer for 5 minutes. Add the mushrooms, peas and sweetcorn, bring back to a simmer, cover and cook for 5–7 minutes. Leave to cool.

2 Place the potatoes in a saucepan, cover with water, bring to the boil and cook for 8 minutes. Drain well and mash with a fork or potato masher. Stir in the yogurt, parsley and seasoning and set aside.

3 Remove the fish from the saucepan using a slotted spoon. Flake the cooked fish away from the skin and place in a gratin dish.

4 Drain the mushrooms, peas and sweetcorn, reserving the cooking liquid. Gently stir into the fish with the salmon strips.

5 Blend a little cooking liquid into the cornflour to make a smooth paste. Transfer the rest of the liquid to a saucepan and add the paste. Heat through, stirring, until thickened. Discard the bay leaves and season.

6 Pour the sauce over the fish and vegetables and stir to mix. Spoon the mashed potato on top and spread to cover, sprinkle with cheese and bake in a preheated oven, 200°C/400°F/ Gas Mark 6, for 25–30 minutes.

pasta & prawn parcels

serves four

450 g/1 lb dried fettuccine

150 ml/5 fl oz Pesto Sauce
   (see page 7)

4 tsp extra virgin olive oil

750 g/1 lb 10 oz large raw prawns,
   peeled and deveined

2 garlic cloves, crushed

125 ml/4 fl oz dry white wine

salt and pepper

wedges of lemon, to garnish

COOK'S TIP

Traditionally, these parcels are
designed to look like money
bags. The resemblance is more
effective with greaseproof paper
than with foil.

1 Cut out 4 squares of greaseproof paper 30 cm/12 inches wide.

2 Bring a large saucepan of lightly salted water to the boil. Add the fettuccine and cook for 2–3 minutes, until just softened. Drain and set aside.

3 Mix the fettuccine with half of the pesto sauce. Spread out the paper squares and place 1 teaspoon of olive oil in the centre of each. Divide the fettuccine between the the squares, then divide the prawns and place on top of the fettuccine.

4 Mix the remaining pesto sauce with the garlic in a small bowl and spoon it over the prawns. Season each parcel with salt and pepper to taste and sprinkle with the white wine.

5 Dampen the edges of the greaseproof paper and bring them together to wrap the parcels loosely, twisting the edges to seal.

6 Place the parcels on a baking tray and bake in a preheated oven, 200°C/400°F/Gas Mark 6, for 10–15 minutes, until piping hot and the prawns have changed colour. Transfer the parcels to serving plates, garnish with lemon wedges and serve.

macaroni & prawn bake

serves four

350 g/12 oz short pasta shapes,
    such as short-cut macaroni
1 tbsp olive oil, plus extra
    for brushing
6 tbsp butter, plus extra for greasing
2 small fennel bulbs, sliced thinly,
    leaves reserved
175 g/6 oz mushrooms, sliced thinly
175 g/6 oz peeled, cooked prawns
600 ml/1 pint hot Béchamel Sauce
    (see page 206)
pinch of cayenne pepper
55 g/2 oz freshly grated
    Parmesan cheese
2 large tomatoes, sliced
1 tsp dried oregano
salt

1 Bring a large saucepan of lightly salted water to the boil. Add the pasta and olive oil, bring back to the boil and cook for 8–10 minutes, or until just tender but still firm to the bite. Drain the pasta, return to the saucepan and dot with 2 tablespoons of the butter. Shake the saucepan well to coat the pasta, cover and keep warm.

2 Melt the remaining butter in a large frying pan over a medium heat, add the sliced fennel and cook for 3–4 minutes, stirring occasionally, until it begins to soften. Stir in the mushrooms and cook for 2 minutes. Stir in the cooked prawns, remove the frying pan from the heat and set aside until required.

3 Season the hot béchamel sauce to taste with a pinch of cayenne. Stir the reserved fennel, mushroom and prawn mixture into the sauce, then stir in the pasta.

4 Grease a round, shallow ovenproof dish with butter. Pour in the pasta mixture and spread evenly. Sprinkle with the Parmesan cheese and arrange the tomato slices in a ring around the edge of the dish. Brush the tomato with olive oil and sprinkle with the dried oregano.

5 Bake in a preheated oven, 180°C/350°F/Gas Mark 4, for 25 minutes, or until golden. Serve hot.

SAVOURY MEALS

seafood lasagne

serves four

450 g/1 lb finnan haddock fillet,
    skin removed and flesh flaked

115 g/4 oz prawns

115 g/4 oz sole fillet, skin removed
    and flesh sliced

juice of 1 lemon

4 tbsp butter

3 leeks, sliced very thinly

6 tbsp plain flour

about 600 ml/1 pint milk

2 tbsp clear honey

200g/7 oz mozzarella cheese, grated

450g/1 lb pre-cooked lasagne

55 g/2 oz freshly grated
    Parmesan cheese

pepper

1 Put the haddock, prawns and sole into a large mixing bowl and season with pepper and lemon juice according to taste. Set aside while you make the sauce.

2 Melt the butter in a large saucepan over a low heat. Add the leeks and cook, stirring occasionally, for 8 minutes, until softened, then add the flour and cook, stirring constantly, for 1 minute. Gradually stir in enough milk to make a thick, creamy sauce.

3 Blend in the clear honey and mozzarella cheese and cook the sauce for a further 3 minutes, then remove the saucepan from the heat and mix in the seasoned haddock, sole and prawn mixture.

4 Place a layer of fish sauce in an ovenproof dish, followed by a layer of lasagne, and continue with alternate layers, finishing with a layer of fish sauce on top. Generously sprinkle over the Parmesan cheese and bake in a preheated oven, 180°C/ 350°F/Gas Mark 4, for 30 minutes. Serve immediately.

VARIATION

For a cider sauce, substitute 1 finely chopped shallot for the leeks, 300 ml/10 fl oz cider and 300 ml/10 fl oz double cream for the milk and 1 teaspoon of mustard for the honey. For a Tuscan sauce, substitute 1 chopped fennel bulb for the leeks and omit the honey.

smoked haddock casserole

serves four

2 tbsp butter, plus extra for greasing

450 g/1 lb smoked haddock fillets,
   cut into 4 portions

600 ml/1 pint milk

2½ tbsp plain flour

pinch of freshly grated nutmeg

3 tbsp double cream

1 tbsp chopped fresh parsley

2 eggs, hard-boiled and mashed
   to a pulp

450 g/1 lb dried fusilli pasta

1 tbsp lemon juice

salt and pepper

fresh flat-leaved parsley, to garnish

TO SERVE

boiled new potatoes

beetroot

VARIATION

Try using penne, conchiglie or
rigatoni for this casserole.

1 Generously grease a casserole with butter. Put the haddock in the casserole and pour over the milk. Bake in a preheated oven, 200°C/400°F/Gas Mark 6, for 15 minutes.

2 Carefully pour off the cooking liquid into a jug without breaking up the fish fillets and reserve. Leave the haddock in the casserole.

3 Melt the butter in a saucepan and stir in the flour. Gradually whisk in the reserved cooking liquid. Season to taste with salt, pepper and nutmeg. Stir in the cream, chopped parsley and mashed hard-boiled eggs and cook, stirring constantly, for 2 minutes.

4 Meanwhile, bring a large saucepan of lightly salted water to the boil. Add the fusilli and the lemon juice, bring back to the boil and cook for 8–10 minutes, until tender but still firm to the bite.

5 Drain the pasta and spoon or tip it over the fish. Top with the egg sauce and return the casserole to the oven for 10 minutes.

6 Transfer the casserole to serving plates, garnish with flat-leaved parsley and serve with boiled new potatoes and beetroot.

fresh baked sardines

serves four

2 tbsp olive oil

2 large onions, sliced into rings

3 garlic cloves, chopped

2 large courgettes, cut into sticks

3 tbsp fresh thyme leaves

8 sardine fillets or about

    1 kg/2 lb 4 oz sardines, filleted

100 g/3½ oz freshly grated

    Parmesan cheese

4 eggs, beaten

300 ml/10 fl oz milk

salt and pepper

VARIATION

If you cannot find sardines that
are large enough to fillet, use
small mackerel instead.

---

1 Heat 1 tablespoon of the olive oil in a frying pan. Add the onions and garlic and cook over a low heat, stirring occasionally, for 2–3 minutes until soft and translucent.

2 Add the courgettes to the frying pan and cook, stirring occasionally, for about 5 minutes, or until turning golden. Stir 2 tablespoons of the thyme leaves into the mixture and remove from the heat.

3 Place half of the onion and courgette mixture in the base of a large ovenproof dish. Top with the sardine fillets and half of the Parmesan cheese. Place the remaining onions and courgettes on top and sprinkle with the remaining thyme.

4 Mix the eggs and milk together in a bowl and season to taste with salt and pepper. Pour the mixture into the dish and sprinkle the remaining Parmesan cheese over the top.

5 Bake in a preheated oven, 180°C/350°F/Gas Mark 4, for 20–25 minutes, or until golden and set. Serve the sardines hot.

trout with smoked bacon

serves four

1 tbsp butter, for greasing

4 whole trout, about 275 g/9½ oz
   each, gutted and cleaned

12 anchovies in oil, drained
   and chopped

2 apples, peeled, cored and sliced

4 fresh mint sprigs

juice of 1 lemon

12 slices of rindless smoked
   streaky bacon

450 g/1 lb dried tagliatelle

1 tbsp olive oil

salt and pepper

TO GARNISH

2 apples, cored and sliced

4 fresh mint sprigs

1 Grease a deep baking tray with the butter.

2 Open up the cavities of each trout and rinse with warm salt water.

3 Season each cavity with salt and pepper. Divide the anchovies, sliced apples and mint sprigs between each of the cavities. Sprinkle with lemon juice.

4 Carefully wrap 3 slices of smoked bacon around the whole of each trout, except the head and tail, in a spiral. Tuck the loose ends of the bacon underneath to secure them.

5 Arrange the trout on the prepared baking tray. Season with pepper. Bake in a preheated oven, 200°C/400°F/Gas Mark 6, for 20 minutes, turning the trout over after 10 minutes.

6 Meanwhile, bring a large saucepan of lightly salted water to the boil. Add the tagliatelle and olive oil and cook for about 12 minutes, until tender but still firm to the bite. Drain the pasta and transfer to a warmed serving dish.

7 Remove the trout from the oven and arrange on the tagliatelle. Garnish with sliced apples and fresh mint sprigs and serve immediately.

spaghetti alla bucaniera

serves four

85 g/3 oz plain flour

450 g/1 lb brill or sole fillets, skinned and chopped

450 g/1 lb hake fillets, skinned and chopped

6 tbsp butter

4 shallots, chopped finely

2 garlic cloves, crushed

1 carrot, diced

1 leek, chopped finely

300 ml/10 fl oz dry cider

300 ml/10 fl oz medium sweet cider

2 tsp anchovy essence

1 tbsp tarragon vinegar

450 g/1 lb dried spaghetti

1 tbsp olive oil

salt and pepper

chopped fresh parsley, to garnish

crusty brown bread, to serve

1 Season the flour with salt and pepper. Sprinkle 25 g/1 oz of the seasoned flour on to a shallow plate. Gently press the fish pieces into the seasoned flour to coat thoroughly all over. Alternatively, put the flour in a plastic bag, add the fish pieces, a few at a time, and shake gently.

2 Melt the butter in a flameproof casserole. Add the fish fillets, shallots, garlic, carrot and leek and cook over a low heat, stirring frequently, for about 10 minutes.

3 Sprinkle over the remaining seasoned flour and cook, stirring constantly, for 2 minutes. Gradually stir in the cider, anchovy essence and tarragon vinegar and bring to the boil. Cover the casserole and transfer to a preheated oven, 180°C/350°F/Gas Mark 4. Bake for 30 minutes.

4 About 15 minutes before the end of the cooking time, bring a large saucepan of lightly salted water to the boil. Add the spaghetti and olive oil, bring back to the boil and cook for about 12 minutes, until tender but still firm to the bite. Drain the pasta thoroughly and transfer to a large, warmed serving dish.

5 Arrange the baked fish mixture on top of the spaghetti and pour over any remaining sauce. Garnish with parsley and serve immediately with warm, crusty brown bread.

cannelloni filetti di sogliola

serves six

12 small fillets of sole, about
115 g/4 oz each
150 ml/5 fl oz red wine
6 tbsp butter
115 g/4 oz button mushrooms, sliced
4 shallots, chopped finely
115 g/4 oz tomatoes, chopped
2 tbsp tomato purée
6 tbsp plain flour, sieved
150 ml/5 fl oz warm milk
2 tbsp double cream
6 dried cannelloni tubes
175 g/6 oz cooked, peeled
freshwater prawns
salt and pepper
1 fresh fennel frond, to garnish

1 Brush the sole fillets with a little wine, season with salt and pepper and roll up, skin side inwards. Secure with a cocktail stick or skewer.

2 Arrange the fish rolls in a single layer in a large frying pan, add the remaining red wine and poach for 4 minutes. Remove from the frying pan and reserve the liquid.

3 Melt the butter in a separate saucepan. Add the mushrooms and shallots and cook for 2 minutes, then add the tomatoes and tomato purée. Season the flour and stir it into the pan. Stir in the reserved cooking liquid and half of the milk. Cook over a low heat, stirring, for 4 minutes. Remove from the heat and stir in the cream.

4 Bring a saucepan of lightly salted water to the boil. Add the cannelloni and cook for about 8 minutes, until tender but still firm to the bite. Drain and leave to cool.

5 Remove the cocktail sticks or skewers from the fish rolls. Put 2 fish rolls into each cannelloni tube, with 2 or 3 prawns and a little red wine sauce. Arrange the cannelloni in a single later in a large ovenproof dish, pour over the red wine sauce and bake in a preheated oven, 200°C/400°F/ Gas Mark 6, for 20 minutes, until cooked through and piping hot.

6 Serve the cannelloni with the red wine sauce, garnished with the remaining prawns and a fennel frond.

orange mackerel

serves four

2 tbsp vegetable oil

4 spring onions, chopped

2 oranges

50 g/1¾ oz ground almonds

1 tbsp oats

50 g/1¾ oz mixed stoned green and
    black olives, chopped

8 mackerel fillets

salt and pepper

crisp salad, to serve

1 Heat the oil in a frying pan. Add
the spring onions and cook
over a low heat for 2 minutes, stirring
frequently, then set aside.

2 Finely grate the rind of the
oranges, then, using a sharp
knife, cut away the remaining skin
and the white pith.

3 Using a sharp knife, segment the
oranges by cutting down either
side of the membrane to loosen each
segment. Do this over a plate so that
you can catch and reserve any juices.
Cut each orange segment in half.

4 Lightly toast the almonds under
a preheated medium grill for
2–3 minutes, or until golden; watch
them carefully as they brown quickly.

5 Mix the spring onions, orange
rind and segments, ground
almonds, oats and olives together in a
bowl and season with salt and pepper.

6 Lay the mackerel fillets in an
ovenproof dish. Spoon the orange
mixture along the centre of each, then
roll up and secure with cocktail sticks.

7 Bake in a preheated oven,
190°C/375°F/Gas Mark 5, for
25 minutes, until the fish is tender.

8 Transfer to serving plates, remove
and discard the cocktail sticks and
serve warm with a salad.

italian cod

serves four

2 tbsp butter

50 g/1¾ oz fresh
  wholemeal breadcrumbs

25 g/1 oz chopped walnuts

grated rind and juice of 2 lemons

2 fresh rosemary sprigs,
  stalks removed

2 tbsp chopped fresh parsley

4 cod fillets, about 150 g/5½ oz each

1 garlic clove, crushed

1 small fresh red chilli, deseeded
  and diced

3 tbsp walnut oil

salad leaves, to serve

VARIATION

If preferred, the walnuts may
be omitted from the crust. In
addition, extra virgin olive oil
can be used instead of walnut
oil, if you wish.

1 Melt the butter in a large
saucepan over a low heat.

2 Remove the saucepan from the
heat and stir in the breadcrumbs
and walnuts, the rind and juice of 1
lemon, half of the fresh rosemary and
half of the fresh parsley.

3 Line a roasting tin with foil
and place the cod fillets in the tin.
Gently press the breadcrumb mixture
over the top of the fillets

4 Bake in a preheated oven,
200°C/400°F/Gas Mark 6, for
25–30 minutes.

5 Place the garlic, the remaining
lemon rind and juice, rosemary
and parsley in a bowl with the chilli
and mix. Beat in the walnut oil. Drizzle
the dressing over the cod fillets as soon
as they are cooked.

6 Transfer to warmed serving plates
and serve with salad leaves.

seafood pizza

serves four

140 g/5 oz standard pizza base mix

4 tbsp chopped fresh dill, plus extra
to garnish

SAUCE

1 large red pepper

400 g/14 oz canned chopped
tomatoes with onion and herbs

3 tbsp tomato purée

salt and pepper

TOPPING

350 g/12 oz assorted cooked
seafood, thawed if frozen

1 tbsp capers in brine, drained

25 g/1 oz stoned black olives in
brine, drained

25 g/1 oz low-fat mozzarella
cheese, grated

15 g/½ oz freshly grated
Parmesan cheese

1 Place the pizza base mix in a
bowl and stir in the fresh dill.
Make the dough according to the
instructions on the packet.

2 Line a baking tray with baking
paper. Press the herbed pizza
dough into an even round about
25 cm/10 inches wide on the prepared
baking tray, then leave in a warm
place to rise.

3 To make the sauce, halve and
deseed the pepper and arrange
on a grill rack. Cook under a preheated
hot grill for about 8–10 minutes, until
softened and charred. Leave to cool
slightly, then peel off the skin and
chop the flesh.

4 Place the pepper flesh in a
saucepan with the tomatoes.
Bring to the boil, reduce the heat and
simmer for 10 minutes until thickened.
Stir in the tomato purée and season to
taste with salt and pepper.

5 Spread the sauce over the pizza
base and top with the seafood.
Sprinkle over the capers and olives,
top with the cheeses and bake in a
preheated oven, 200°C/400°F/Gas
Mark 6, for 25–30 minutes. Garnish
with fresh dill and serve hot.

COOK'S TIP

Look for packets of prepared
mixed seafood in the chiller
cabinets of large supermarkets.
These have more flavour and a
better texture than frozen.

smoked cod polenta

serves four

1.5 litres/2¾ pints water

350 g/12 oz instant polenta

200 g/7 oz frozen chopped
   spinach, thawed and drained

3 tbsp butter

50 g/1¾ oz pecorino cheese, grated

200 ml/7 fl oz milk

450 g/1 lb smoked cod
   fillet, skinned

4 eggs, beaten

salt and pepper

1 Bring the water to the boil in a large saucepan. Add the polenta and cook, stirring, for 20–25 minutes.

2 Stir the spinach, butter and half of the pecorino cheese into the polenta, then season to taste with salt and pepper.

3 Divide the cooked polenta between 4 individual ovenproof dishes, spreading it evenly across the bases and up the sides of the dishes.

4 Bring the milk to the boil in a frying pan. Add the fish and cook, turning once, for 8–10 minutes, or until tender. Remove the fish with a slotted spoon.

5 Remove the frying pan from the heat. Pour the eggs into the milk in the frying pan and mix together.

VARIATION

Try using 350 g/12 oz of cooked chicken breast with 2 tablespoons chopped tarragon instead of the smoked cod, if you wish.

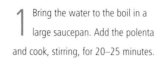

6 Using a fork, flake the fish into smaller pieces and place it in the centre of the ovenproof dishes.

7 Pour the milk and egg mixture over the fish.

8 Sprinkle with the remaining cheese and bake in a preheated oven, 190°C/375°F/Gas Mark 5, for 25–30 minutes, or until set and golden. Serve hot.

fillets of red mullet & pasta

serves four

1 kg/2 lb 4 oz red mullet fillets

300 ml/10 fl oz dry white wine

4 shallots, chopped finely

1 garlic clove, crushed

3 tbsp finely chopped mixed
    fresh herbs

finely grated rind and juice of
    1 lemon

pinch of freshly grated nutmeg

3 anchovy fillets, chopped roughly

2 tbsp double cream

1 tsp cornflour

450 g/1 lb dried vermicelli

1 tbsp olive oil

salt and pepper

TO GARNISH

1 fresh mint sprig

slices of lemon

strips of lemon rind

1 Place the red mullet fillets in a large casserole. Pour over the wine and add the shallots, garlic, herbs, lemon rind and juice, nutmeg and anchovies. Season to taste with salt and pepper. Cover and bake in a preheated oven, 180°C/350°F/Gas Mark 4, for 35 minutes.

2 Lift the mullet out of the casserole with a slotted spoon and transfer to a warmed dish, reserving the cooking liquid. Set the fish aside and keep warm.

3 Pour the cooking liquid into a saucepan and bring to the boil. Simmer for 25 minutes, until reduced by half. Mix the cream and cornflour to a paste and stir into the sauce to thicken.

4 Meanwhile, bring a saucepan of lightly salted water to the boil. Add the vermicelli and oil, bring back to the boil and cook for 8–10 minutes, until tender but still firm to the bite. Drain and transfer to a warmed serving dish.

5 Arrange the red mullet fillets on top of the vermicelli and pour over the sauce. Garnish with a fresh mint sprig, slices of lemon and strips of lemon rind and serve immediately.

italian chicken parcels

serves six

1 tbsp olive oil, for brushing

6 skinless chicken breast fillets

250 g/9 oz mozzarella cheese

500 g/1 lb 2 oz courgettes, sliced

6 large tomatoes, sliced

1 small bunch of fresh basil
or oregano

pepper

rice or pasta, to serve

COOK'S TIP

To aid cooking, place the
vegetables and chicken on the
shiny side of the foil so that once
the parcel is wrapped up, the
dull surface of the foil is facing
outwards. This ensures that the
heat is absorbed into the parcel
and not reflected away.

VARIATION

This recipe also works well with
monkfish fillet. Use 6 x
140–175 g/5–6 oz fillets. Remove
all the grey membrane first.

1 Cut out 6 squares of foil about 25 cm/10 inches wide. Brush the squares lightly with oil and set aside until required.

2 Slash each chicken breast fillet 3–4 times. Slice the cheese and tuck the slices between the slashes.

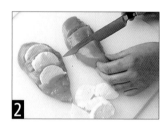

3 Divide the courgettes and tomatoes between the foil squares and season with pepper. Tear or roughly chop the herbs and scatter them over the vegetables.

4 Place the chicken on top of each pile of vegetables, then wrap the foil to enclose the chicken and vegetables, sealing at the edges.

5 Place on a baking tray. Bake in a preheated oven, 200°C/400°C/ Gas Mark 6, for about 30 minutes.

6 Unwrap each foil parcel and serve with rice or pasta.

crispy stuffed chicken

serves four

4 skinless, boneless chicken breasts,
  about 150 g/5½ oz each

4 fresh tarragon sprigs

½ small orange pepper, deseeded
  and sliced

½ small green pepper, deseeded
  and sliced

15 g/½ oz fresh wholemeal
  breadcrumbs

1 tbsp sesame seeds

4 tbsp lemon juice

salt and pepper

fresh tarragon, to garnish

PEPPER SAUCE

1 small red pepper, halved
  and deseeded

200 g/7 oz canned
  chopped tomatoes

1 small fresh red chilli, deseeded
  and chopped

¼ tsp celery salt

salt and pepper

1 Make a slit in each of the chicken breasts with a small, sharp knife to create a pocket. Season inside each pocket with salt and pepper.

2 Place a sprig of tarragon and a few slices of orange pepper and green pepper in each pocket. Place the chicken breasts on a non-stick baking tray and sprinkle the breadcrumbs and sesame seeds over them.

3 Spoon 1 tablespoon of lemon juice over each chicken breast and bake in a preheated oven, 190°C/375°F/Gas Mark 5, for 35–40 minutes, until the chicken is golden brown, tender and cooked through.

4 Meanwhile, arrange the red pepper halves on a grill rack, skin side up, and cook under a preheated hot grill for 5–6 minutes, until the skin starts to char and blister. Leave the grilled pepper to cool for about 10 minutes, then peel off the skin.

5 Place the red pepper in a food processor,, add the tomatoes, chilli and celery salt and process for a few seconds. Season to taste. Alternatively, finely chop the red pepper and press through a sieve with the tomatoes and chilli.

6 When the chicken is cooked, heat the sauce, spoon a little on to each of 4 warmed plates and arrange a chicken breast in the centre of each. Garnish with tarragon and serve.

chicken & spinach lasagne

serves four

350 g/12 oz frozen chopped
  spinach, thawed and drained
½ tsp ground nutmeg
450 g/1 lb lean, cooked chicken
  meat, skinned and diced
4 sheets pre-cooked lasagne verde
1½ tbsp cornflour
425 ml/15 fl oz skimmed milk
70 g/2½ oz freshly grated
  Parmesan cheese
salt and pepper
TOMATO SAUCE
400 g/14 oz canned
  chopped tomatoes
1 onion, chopped finely
1 garlic clove, crushed
150 ml/5 fl oz white wine
3 tbsp tomato purée
1 tsp dried oregano
salt and pepper

1 To make the tomato sauce, place the tomatoes in a saucepan and stir in the onion, garlic, wine, tomato purée and oregano. Bring to the boil and simmer for 20 minutes, stirring occasionally, until thick. Season well with salt and pepper.

2 Drain the spinach again and spread it out on kitchen paper to make sure that as much water as possible is removed. Layer the spinach in the base of an ovenproof dish. Sprinkle with nutmeg and season.

3 Arrange the diced chicken over the spinach and spoon over the tomato sauce. Arrange the sheets of lasagne over the tomato sauce.

4 Blend the cornflour with a little of the milk to make a paste. Pour the remaining milk into a saucepan and stir in the cornflour paste. Heat for 2–3 minutes, stirring, until the sauce thickens. Season well.

5 Pour the sauce over the lasagne and transfer the dish to a baking tray. Sprinkle the Parmesan cheese over the sauce and bake in a preheated oven, 200°C/400°F/Gas Mark 6, for 25 minutes, until golden. Serve hot.

chicken pasta bake

serves four

2 fennel bulbs

2 red onions, sliced very thinly

1 tbsp lemon juice

125 g/4½ oz button mushrooms

1 tbsp olive oil

225 g/8 oz dried penne pasta

55 g/2 oz raisins

225 g/8 oz lean, boneless cooked
    chicken, skinned and shredded

375 g/13 oz low-fat soft cheese
    with garlic and herbs

125 g/4½ oz low-fat mozzarella
    cheese, sliced thinly

35 g/1¼ oz freshly grated
    Parmesan cheese

salt and pepper

1 Trim the fennel bulbs, reserving the green fronds for the garnish, then slice the bulbs thinly.

2 Generously coat the onions in the lemon juice. Cut the mushrooms into quarters.

3 Heat the oil in a large frying pan and cook the fennel, onion and mushrooms for 4–5 minutes, stirring, until just softened. Season well, transfer the mixture to a large bowl and set aside.

4 Bring a saucepan of lightly salted water to the boil, add the pasta and cook for 8–10 minutes, until tender but still firm to the bite. Drain, and mix with the vegetables.

5 Stir the raisins and cooked chicken into the pasta mixture. Beat the soft cheese to soften it further, then mix it into the pasta and chicken – the heat from the pasta should make the cheese melt slightly.

6 Transfer the mixture to an ovenproof dish and place on a baking tray. Arrange slices of mozzarella over the top and sprinkle with the Parmesan cheese.

7 Bake in a preheated oven, 200°C/400°F/Gas Mark 6, for 20–25 minutes, until golden brown.

8 Garnish with chopped fennel fronds and serve hot.

chicken & ham lasagne

serves four

1 tbsp butter, for greasing

14 sheets pre-cooked lasagne

850 ml/1½ pints Béchamel Sauce
   (see page 206)

85 g/3 oz freshly grated
   Parmesan cheese

CHICKEN AND MUSHROOM SAUCE

2 tbsp olive oil

2 garlic cloves, crushed

1 large onion, chopped finely

225 g/8 oz wild mushrooms, sliced

300 g/10½ oz minced chicken

85 g/3 oz chicken livers,
   chopped finely

115 g/4 oz Parma ham, diced

150 ml/5 fl oz Marsala wine

280 g/10 oz canned
   chopped tomatoes

1 tbsp chopped fresh basil leaves

2 tbsp tomato purée

salt and pepper

1 To make the chicken and mushroom sauce, heat the olive oil in a large saucepan. Add the garlic, onion and mushrooms and cook, stirring frequently, for 6 minutes.

2 Add the minced chicken, chicken livers and Parma ham and cook over a low heat, stirring frequently, for about 12 minutes, or until the meat has browned.

3 Stir the Marsala, tomatoes, basil and tomato purée into the mixture in the saucepan and cook for 4 minutes. Season with salt and pepper to taste, cover and simmer gently for 30 minutes, stirring occasionally. Stir thoroughly, then simmer, uncovered, for 15 minutes.

4 Lightly grease an ovenproof dish with the butter. Arrange sheets of lasagne over the base of the dish, spoon over a layer of the chicken and mushroom sauce, then spoon over a layer of the béchamel sauce. Place another layer of lasagne on top and repeat the process twice, finishing with a layer of béchamel sauce. Sprinkle over the Parmesan cheese and bake in a preheated oven, 190°C/ 375°F/Gas Mark 5, for 35 minutes, until golden brown and bubbling. Serve immediately.

chicken lasagne

serves four

9 sheets fresh or dried lasagne

1 tbsp butter. for greasing

1 tbsp olive oil

1 red onion, chopped finely

1 garlic clove, crushed

100 g/3½ oz mushrooms, sliced

350 g/12 oz skinless, boneless
    chicken or turkey breast, cut
    into chunks

150 ml/5 fl oz red wine, diluted
    with 100 ml/3½ fl oz water

250 g/9 oz passata

1 tsp sugar

75 g/2¾ oz freshly grated
    Parmesan cheese

salt

BÉCHAMEL SAUCE

5 tbsp butter

5 tbsp plain flour

600 ml/1 pint milk

1 egg, beaten

salt and pepper

1 Bring a large saucepan of lightly salted water to the boil. Add the lasagne and cook according to the instructions on the packet. Lightly grease a deep ovenproof dish.

2 Place the oil in a frying pan over a low heat. Add the onion and garlic and cook for 3–4 minutes. Add the mushrooms and chicken and stir-fry for 4 minutes, or until the meat browns.

3 Add the diluted wine, bring the mixture to the boil, then reduce the heat and simmer for 5 minutes. Stir in the passata and sugar and cook for 3–5 minutes until the meat is tender and cooked through. The sauce should have thickened, but still be quite runny.

4 To make the béchamel sauce, melt the butter in a saucepan, stir in the flour and cook for 2 minutes. Remove the saucepan from the heat and gradually add the milk, mixing to form a smooth sauce. Return the saucepan to the heat and bring to the boil, stirring until thickened. Leave to cool slightly, then beat in the egg and season. Stir in half of the Parmesan cheese.

5 Place 3 sheets of lasagne in the base of the prepared dish and spread with half of the chicken mixture. Repeat the layers. Top with the last 3 sheets of lasagne, pour over the béchamel sauce and sprinkle with the remaining Parmesan cheese. Bake in a preheated oven, 190°C/375°F/Gas Mark 5, for 30 minutes, until golden and the pasta is cooked. Serve hot.

mustard-baked chicken

serves four

4 large or 8 small chicken pieces

4 tbsp butter, melted

4 tbsp mild mustard (see Cook's Tip)

2 tbsp lemon juice

1 tbsp brown sugar

1 tsp paprika

3 tbsp poppy seeds

400 g/14 oz dried pasta shells

1 tbsp olive oil

salt and pepper

COOK'S TIP

Dijon is the type of mustard most often used in cooking, as it has a clean and only mildly spicy flavour. German mustard has a sweet-sour taste, although Bavarian mustard is slightly sweeter. American mustard is mild and sweet.

VARIATION

This recipe would also work well with a variety of feathered game, such as guinea fowl and young pheasant.

1 Arrange the chicken pieces in a single layer in the base of a large ovenproof dish.

2 Mix the butter, mustard, lemon juice, brown sugar and paprika together in a bowl and season with salt and pepper to taste. Brush the mixture over the upper surfaces of the chicken pieces and bake in a preheated oven, 200°C/400°F/Gas Mark 6, for 15 minutes.

3 Remove the dish from the oven and carefully turn over the chicken. Coat the upper surfaces of the chicken pieces with the remaining mustard mixture, sprinkle over the poppy seeds and return to the oven for a further 15 minutes.

4 Meanwhile, bring a large saucepan of lightly salted water to the boil. Add the pasta shells and olive oil, bring back to the boil and cook for 8–10 minutes, or until tender but still firm to the bite.

5 Drain the pasta thoroughly and divide between 4 warmed serving plates. Top the pasta with 1 or 2 of the chicken pieces, pour over the sauce and serve immediately.

roast duckling with apple

serves four

4 duckling pieces, about
    350 g/12 oz each
4 tbsp dark soy sauce
2 tbsp light muscovado sugar
2 red-skinned apples
2 green-skinned apples
juice of 1 lemon
2 tbsp clear honey
a few bay leaves
salt and pepper
a selection of fresh vegetables,
    to serve
APRICOT SAUCE
400 g/14 oz canned apricots in
    fruit juice
4 tbsp sweet sherry

1 Wash the duckling and trim away any excess fat. Place on a wire rack over a roasting tin and prick all over with a fork.

2 Brush the duck with the soy sauce. Sprinkle over the sugar and season with pepper. Cook in a preheated oven, 190°C/375°F/Gas Mark 5, basting occasionally, for 50–60 minutes, until the meat is cooked through – the juices should run clear when a skewer is inserted into the thickest part of the meat.

3 Meanwhile, core the apples and cut each of them into 6 wedges. Mix with the lemon juice and honey in a bowl. Place the fruit and liquid in a

small roasting tin. Add a few bay leaves and season. Cook alongside the duckling, basting occasionally, for 20–25 minutes, until tender. Discard the bay leaves.

4 To make the sauce, place the apricots and their juices in a food processor with the sherry and process into a purée. Alternatively, mash the apricots with a fork until smooth and mix with the juice and sherry.

5 Just before serving, heat the apricot sauce in a small saucepan. Remove the skin from the duckling and pat the flesh with kitchen paper to absorb any fat. Serve the duckling with the apple wedges, apricot sauce and fresh vegetables.

pesto-baked partridge

serves four

8 partridge pieces, 115 g/4 oz each

4 tbsp butter, melted

4 tbsp Dijon mustard

2 tbsp lime juice

1 tbsp brown sugar

6 tbsp Pesto Sauce (see page 7)

450 g/1 lb dried rigatoni pasta

1 tbsp olive oil

115 g/4 oz freshly grated
    Parmesan cheese

salt and pepper

VARIATION

You could also prepare young
pheasant in the same way.

---

1 Arrange the partridge pieces,
smooth side down, in a single
layer in a large, ovenproof dish.

2 Mix the butter, Dijon mustard,
lime juice and brown sugar
together in a bowl. Season to taste
with salt and pepper. Brush the mixture
over the partridge pieces, reserving the
remaining mixture, and bake in a
preheated oven, 200°C/400°F/
Gas Mark 6, for 15 minutes.

3 Remove the dish from the oven
and coat the partridge pieces
with 3 tablespoons of the pesto sauce.
Return to the oven and bake for a
further 12 minutes.

4 Remove the dish from the oven
and carefully turn over the
partridge pieces. Coat the top of the
partridge with the remaining mustard
mixture and return to the oven for a
further 10 minutes.

5 Meanwhile, bring a large
saucepan of lightly salted water
to the boil. Add the rigatoni and olive
oil and cook for 8–10 minutes, until
tender but still firm to the bite. Drain
and transfer to a serving dish.

6 Add the remaining pesto sauce
and the Parmesan cheese to the
pasta and toss thoroughly to blend.
Transfer the partridge to serving plates
and serve with the pasta, pouring over
the cooking juices.

honey-glazed duck

serves four

2 large boneless duck breasts,
  about 225g/8 oz each

MARINADE

1 tsp dark soy sauce

2 tbsp clear honey

1 tsp garlic vinegar

2 garlic cloves, crushed

1 tsp ground star anise

2 tsp cornflour

2 tsp water

TO GARNISH

celery leaves

cucumber wedges

fresh chives

COOK'S TIP

If the duck begins to burn
slightly while it is cooking,
cover with foil. Check that
the duck breasts are cooked
through by inserting the point
of a sharp knife into the thickest
part of the meat – the juices
should run clear.

1 To make the marinade, mix the soy sauce, honey, garlic vinegar, garlic and star anise together in a bowl. Blend the cornflour with the water to form a smooth paste and stir it into the mixture.

2 Place the duck in a shallow dish. Brush the marinade over the top, turning the meat to coat. Cover and leave to marinate in the refrigerator for at least 2 hours, or overnight.

3 Drain the duck, reserving the marinade. Place in a shallow ovenproof dish and bake in a preheated oven, 220°C/425°F/Gas Mark 7, for 20–25 minutes, basting frequently with the marinade.

4 Remove the duck from the oven. Transfer to a preheated medium grill and grill for about 3–4 minutes to caramelize the top, without charring.

5 Remove the duck from the grill pan and cut it into thin slices. Arrange the slices on a warmed serving dish, garnish with celery leaves, cucumber wedges and fresh chives and serve immediately.

red roast pork in soy sauce

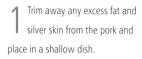

serves four

450 g/1 lb lean pork fillet

MARINADE

6 tbsp dark soy sauce

2 tbsp dry sherry

1 tsp Chinese five-spice powder

2 garlic cloves, crushed

2 tsp finely chopped fresh root ginger

1 large red pepper

1 large yellow pepper

1 large orange pepper

4 tbsp caster sugar

2 tbsp red wine vinegar

TO GARNISH

shredded spring onions

snipped fresh chives

1 Trim away any excess fat and silver skin from the pork and place in a shallow dish.

2 To make the marinade, mix the soy sauce, sherry, Chinese five-spice powder, garlic and ginger together in a bowl. Spoon over the pork, turning it to coat. Cover and marinate in the refrigerator for at least 1 hour, or until required.

3 Drain the pork, reserving the marinade. Place the pork on a roasting rack over a roasting tin. Cook in a preheated oven, 190°C/375°F/ Gas Mark 5, basting occasionally with the marinade, for 1 hour, or until cooked through.

4 Meanwhile, halve and deseed the red, yellow and orange peppers. Cut each pepper half into 3 equal portions. Arrange them on a baking tray and bake alongside the pork for the last 30 minutes of cooking time.

5 Place the sugar and vinegar in a saucepan and heat gently until the sugar dissolves. Bring to the boil and simmer for 3–4 minutes, until syrupy.

6 When the pork is cooked, remove it from the oven and brush with the sugar syrup. Leave to stand for about 5 minutes, then slice and arrange on a serving platter with the peppers. Garnish with shredded spring onions and snipped fresh chives and serve.

braised fennel & linguine

serves four

6 fennel bulbs

150 ml/5 fl oz Vegetable Stock
(see page 7)

2 tbsp butter

6 slices rindless smoked
bacon, diced

6 shallots, quartered

2½ tbsp plain flour

100 ml/3½ fl oz double cream

1 tbsp Madeira

450 g/1 lb dried linguine pasta

1 tbsp olive oil

salt and pepper

1 Trim the fennel bulbs, then peel off and reserve the outer layer of each. Cut the bulbs into quarters and put them in a large saucepan with the stock and the reserved outer layers.

2 Bring to the boil, lower the heat and simmer for 5 minutes.

3 Using a slotted spoon, transfer the fennel to a large dish, discarding the outer layers of the bulbs. Bring the stock to the boil and allow to reduce by half. Set aside.

4 Melt the butter in a frying pan over a low heat. Add the bacon and shallots and cook, stirring frequently, for 4 minutes. Add the flour, reduced stock, cream and Madeira and cook, stirring constantly, for 3 minutes, or until the sauce is smooth. Season to taste with salt and pepper and pour over the fennel.

5 Bring a large saucepan of lightly salted water to the boil. Add the pasta and olive oil, bring back to the boil and cook for 8–10 minutes, until tender but still firm to the bite. Drain and transfer to a deep ovenproof dish.

6 Add the fennel and sauce. Braise in a preheated oven, 180°C/ 350°F/Gas Mark 4, for 20 minutes. Serve immediately.

stuffed cannelloni

serves four

8 dried cannelloni tubes

1 tbsp olive oil

25 g/1 oz freshly grated
　Parmesan cheese

fresh flat-leaved parsley sprigs,
　to garnish

FILLING

2 tbsp butter

300 g/10½ oz frozen chopped
　spinach, thawed and drained

115 g/4 oz ricotta cheese

25 g/1 oz freshly grated
　Parmesan cheese

55 g/2 oz chopped ham

pinch of freshly grated nutmeg

2 tbsp double cream

2 eggs, lightly beaten

salt and pepper

SAUCE

2 tbsp butter

2½ tbsp plain flour

300 ml/10 fl oz milk

2 bay leaves

pinch of freshly grated nutmeg

salt and pepper

1 To make the filling, melt the butter in a saucepan, add the spinach and stir-fry for 2–3 minutes. Remove from the heat, transfer to an ovenproof bowl and stir in the ricotta, Parmesan cheese and ham. Season to taste with nutmeg, salt and pepper. Beat in the cream and eggs to make a thick paste.

2 Bring a large saucepan of lightly salted water to the boil. Add the cannelloni and the oil and cook for 10–12 minutes, or until almost tender. Drain and leave to cool.

3 To make the sauce, melt the butter in a pan. Stir in the flour and cook, stirring, for 1 minute. Gradually stir in the milk. Add the bay leaves and simmer, stirring, for 5 minutes. Add the nutmeg and salt and pepper to taste. Remove from the heat and discard the bay leaves.

4 Spoon the filling into a piping bag and fill the cooked cannelloni.

5 Spoon a little sauce into the base of an ovenproof dish. Arrange the cannelloni in the dish in a single layer and pour over the remaining sauce. Sprinkle over the Parmesan cheese and bake in a preheated oven, 190°C/ 375°F/Gas Mark 5, for 40–45 minutes. Garnish with sprigs of fresh flat-leaved parsley and serve.

italian calzone

serves four

1 quantity Basic Pizza Dough
(see page 6)

plain flour for dusting

1 egg, beaten

FILLING

1 tbsp tomato purée

25 g/1 oz Italian salami, chopped

25 g/1 oz mortadella, chopped

1 tomato, peeled and chopped

25 g/1 oz ricotta cheese

2 spring onions, chopped

¼ tsp dried oregano

salt and pepper

fresh flat-leaved parsley, to garnish

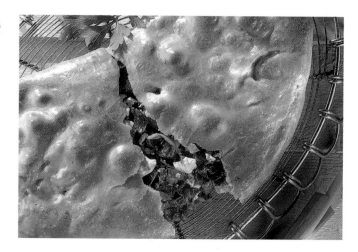

1 Knead the dough and roll out on a lightly floured work surface into a 23-cm/9-inch round.

2 Brush the edges of the dough with a little beaten egg. Reserve the remaining egg.

3 Spread the tomato purée over the half of the round nearest to you.

4 Scatter the salami, mortadella and chopped tomato on top.

5 Dot with the ricotta and sprinkle over the spring onions and oregano. Season to taste.

6 Fold over the uncovered half of the dough to form a semicircle. Press the edges of the dough firmly together to prevent the filling from leaking out during cooking.

7 Transfer the calzone to a baking tray and brush with beaten egg to glaze. Make a hole in the top to allow steam to escape during cooking.

8 Bake in a preheated oven, 200°C/400°F/Gas Mark 6, for 20 minutes, or until golden. Transfer the cooked calzone to a warmed serving platter, garnish with flat-leaved parsley and serve immediately.

aubergine pasta cake

serves four

1 tbsp butter, for greasing

1 aubergine

300 g/10½ oz tricolour
    pasta shapes

125 g/4½ oz low-fat soft cheese
    with garlic and herbs

350 ml/12 fl oz passata

70 g/2½ oz freshly grated
    Parmesan cheese

1½ tsp dried oregano

25 g/1 oz dried white breadcrumbs

salt and pepper

fresh oregano sprigs, to garnish

1 Grease a 20-cm/8-inch round springform cake tin and line with baking paper.

2 Trim the aubergine and cut it lengthways into slices about 5 mm/¼ inch thick. Place in a bowl, sprinkle with salt and leave to stand for 30 minutes to remove any bitter juices. Rinse under cold running water.

3 Bring a saucepan of water to the boil and blanch the aubergine slices for 1 minute. Drain and pat dry with kitchen paper. Set aside.

4 Bring a separate, large saucepan of lightly salted water to the boil. Add the pasta shapes, return to the boil and cook for 8–10 minutes, until tender but still firm to the bite. Drain well and return to the saucepan. Add the soft cheese and allow it to melt over the pasta.

5 Stir in the passata, Parmesan cheese and oregano and season with salt and pepper.

6 Arrange the aubergine slices over the base and sides of the cake tin, overlapping the slices and making sure there are no gaps.

7 Pile the pasta mixture into the tin, packing it down well, and sprinkle with the breadcrumbs. Bake in

a preheated oven, 190°C/375°F/Gas Mark 5, for 20 minutes, then leave to stand for 15 minutes.

8 Loosen the cake around the edge of the tin with a palette knife and turn it out, aubergine side uppermost. Garnish with oregano and serve hot.

pasticcio

serves six

225 g/8 oz fusilli, or other short
    pasta shapes

1 tbsp olive oil, plus extra
    for brushing

4 tbsp double cream

salt

fresh rosemary sprigs, to garnish

BEEF SAUCE

2 tbsp olive oil

1 onion, sliced thinly

1 red pepper, deseeded
    and chopped

2 garlic cloves, chopped

625 g/1 lb 6 oz lean minced beef

400 g/14 oz canned
    chopped tomatoes

125 ml/4 fl oz dry white wine

2 tbsp chopped fresh parsley

50 g/1¾ oz canned anchovies,
    drained and chopped

salt and pepper

TOPPING

300 ml/10 fl oz natural yogurt

3 eggs

pinch of freshly grated nutmeg

40 g/1½ oz freshly grated
    Parmesan cheese

salt and pepper

1 To make the sauce, heat the oil in a large frying pan, add the onion and red pepper and cook for 3 minutes. Stir in the garlic and cook for 1 minute. Stir in the beef and cook, stirring frequently, until browned.

2 Add the tomatoes and wine and stir well. Bring to the boil, then simmer, uncovered, for 20 minutes, or until the sauce is fairly thick. Stir in the parsley and anchovies and season.

3 Bring a large saucepan of salted water to the boil, add the pasta and oil and cook for 8–10 minutes, or until tender but still firm to the bite Drain, then transfer to a bowl. Stir in the cream and set aside.

4 To make the topping, beat together the yogurt, eggs and nutmeg until well blended and season with salt and pepper to taste.

5 Brush a large, shallow ovenproof dish with oil. Spoon in half of the pasta mixture and cover with half of the beef sauce. Repeat the layers, then spread the topping evenly over the final layer. Sprinkle the grated Parmesan cheese evenly on top.

6 Bake in a preheated oven, 190°C/375°F/Gas Mark 5, for 25 minutes, or until the topping is golden brown and bubbling. Garnish with fresh rosemary and serve.

hot pot chops

serves four

4 lean, boneless lamb leg steaks,
  about 125 g/4½ oz each

1 small onion, sliced thinly

1 carrot, sliced thinly

1 potato, sliced thinly

1 tsp olive oil

1 tsp dried rosemary

salt and pepper

fresh rosemary, to garnish

freshly steamed green vegetables,
  to serve

1 Trim any excess fat from the lamb steaks using a small, sharp knife.

2 Season both sides of the steaks with salt and pepper to taste and arrange them on a baking tray.

3 Alternate layers of sliced onion, carrot and potato on top of each steak, finishing with a layer of potato.

4 Brush the top layer of potato lightly with oil, season with salt and pepper to taste, then sprinkle with a little dried rosemary.

5 Place the hot pot chops in a preheated oven, 180°C/350°F/ Gas Mark 4, and bake for 25–30 minutes, until the lamb is tender and cooked through.

6 Drain the lamb steaks on kitchen paper and transfer to a warmed serving plate.

7 Garnish with fresh rosemary and serve accompanied by freshly steamed green vegetables.

fruity lamb casserole

serves four

450 g/1 lb lean lamb, trimmed and
   cut into 2.5-cm/1-inch cubes

1 tsp ground cinnamon

1 tsp ground coriander

1 tsp ground cumin

2 tsp olive oil

1 red onion, chopped finely

1 garlic clove, crushed

400 g/14 oz canned
   chopped tomatoes

2 tbsp tomato purée

125 g/4½ oz no-soak dried apricots

1 tsp caster sugar

300 ml/10 fl oz Vegetable Stock
   (see page 7)

salt and pepper

1 small bunch of fresh coriander,
   to garnish

rice or steamed couscous, to serve

1 Place the lamb in a mixing bowl and add the cinnamon, coriander, cumin and oil. Mix thoroughly to coat the lamb in the spices.

2 Place a non-stick frying pan over a high heat for a few seconds until hot, then add the spiced lamb, reduce the heat and cook for 4–5 minutes, stirring, until browned all over. Remove the lamb using a slotted spoon and transfer to a large ovenproof casserole.

3 Add the onion, garlic, tomatoes and tomato purée to the frying pan and cook, stirring occasionally, for 5 minutes. Season to taste with salt and pepper. Stir in the dried apricots and sugar, add the stock and bring to the boil.

4 Spoon the sauce over the lamb and mix well. Cover and cook in a preheated oven, 180°C/350°F/Gas Mark 4, for 1 hour, removing the lid of the casserole for the last 10 minutes.

5 Roughly chop the coriander and sprinkle over the casserole to garnish. Serve immediately with rice or steamed couscous.

223

fresh spaghetti & meatballs

serves four

150 g/5½ oz fresh wholemeal
    breadcrumbs

150 ml/5 fl oz milk

1 large onion, chopped

450 g/1 lb minced steak

1 tsp paprika

4 tbsp olive oil

1 tbsp butter

450 g/1 lb fresh spaghetti

salt and pepper

fresh tarragon sprigs, to garnish

TOMATO SAUCE

1 tbsp butter

2½ tbsp wholemeal flour

200 ml/7 fl oz beef stock

400 g/14 oz canned
    chopped tomatoes

2 tbsp tomato purée

1 tsp sugar

1 tbsp finely chopped fresh tarragon

salt and pepper

1 Place the breadcrumbs in a bowl, add the milk and leave to soak for about 30 minutes.

2 To make the tomato sauce, melt the butter in a saucepan. Add the flour and cook, stirring constantly, for 2 minutes. Gradually stir in the beef stock and cook, stirring constantly, for a further 5 minutes. Add the tomatoes, tomato purée, sugar and tarragon. Season and simmer for 25 minutes.

3 Mix the onion, steak and paprika into the breadcrumbs and season with salt and pepper to taste. Shape the mixture into 14 meatballs.

4 Heat the oil and butter in a frying pan over a low heat, add the meatballs and cook, turning, until browned. Place in a deep casserole, pour over the tomato sauce, cover and bake in a preheated oven, 180°C/ 350°F/ Gas Mark 4, for 25 minutes.

5 Bring a large saucepan of lightly salted water to the boil. Add the fresh spaghetti, bring back to the boil and cook for about 2–3 minutes, or until tender but still firm to the bite.

6 Meanwhile, remove the meatballs from the oven and leave to cool for 3 minutes. Drain the spaghetti and transfer to a serving dish, then pour the meatballs and sauce over the top. Garnish with tarragon and serve.

meatballs in red wine sauce

serves four

150 g/5½ oz fresh
   white breadcrumbs

150 ml/5 fl oz milk

12 shallots, chopped

450 g/1 lb minced steak

1 tsp paprika

5 tbsp olive oil

1 tbsp butter

450 g/1 lb dried egg tagliatelli pasta

salt and pepper

fresh basil sprigs, to garnish

MUSHROOM AND WINE SAUCE

1 tbsp butter

4 tbsp olive oil

225 g/8 oz sliced oyster mushrooms

2½ tbsp wholemeal flour

200 ml/7 fl oz beef stock

150 ml/5 fl oz red wine

4 tomatoes, peeled and chopped

1 tbsp tomato purée

1 tsp brown sugar

1 tbsp finely chopped fresh basil

salt and pepper

1 Place the breadcrumbs in a bowl, add the milk and leave to soak for about 30 minutes.

2 To make the sauce, heat the butter and oil in a saucepan. Add the mushrooms and cook for 4 minutes. Stir in the flour and cook for 2 minutes. Add the stock and wine and simmer for 15 minutes. Add the tomatoes, tomato purée, sugar and basil. Season and simmer for 30 minutes.

3 Mix the shallots, steak and paprika with the breadcrumbs and season to taste. Shape the mixture into 14 meatballs.

4 Heat 4 tablespoons of the oil and the butter in a large frying pan over a medium heat. Add the meatballs and cook, turning, until browned. Transfer the meatballs to a deep casserole and pour over the mushroom and wine sauce. Cover and bake in a preheated oven, 180°C/350°F/Gas Mark 4, for 30 minutes.

5 Bring a saucepan of lightly salted water to the boil. Add the pasta and the remaining oil, bring back to the boil and cook for 8–10 minutes, or until tender but still firm to the bite. Drain and transfer to a serving dish.

6 Remove the casserole from the oven and leave to cool for 3 minutes. Pour the meatballs and sauce over the pasta, garnish with sprigs of basil and serve.

lasagne verde

serves six

Ragù Sauce (see page 6)

1 tbsp olive oil

225 g/8 oz lasagne verde

1 tbsp butter, for greasing

Béchamel Sauce (see page 206)

55 g/2oz freshly grated
    Parmesan cheese

salt and pepper

green salad, tomato salad or
    black olives, to serve

1 Make the ragù sauce as described on page 6, but cook for 10–12 minutes longer than the time given, uncovered, to allow the excess liquid to evaporate. The sauce needs to be reduced to the consistency of a thick paste.

2 Bring a large saucepan of lightly salted water to the boil and add the olive oil. Drop the lasagne sheets into the boiling water a few at a time, bringing back to the boil before adding further sheets to the saucepan. If you are using fresh lasagne sheets, cook them for 8 minutes; if you are using dried or partly pre-cooked lasagne, cook according to the instructions on the packet.

3 Remove the lasagne sheets from the saucepan with a slotted spoon. Spread them out in a single layer on clean, damp tea towels.

4 Grease a rectangular ovenproof dish measuring about 25–28 cm/ 10–11 inches long. Spoon a little of the ragù sauce into the base of the prepared dish, cover with a layer of lasagne, then spoon over a little of the béchamel sauce and sprinkle with some of the Parmesan cheese. Repeat the layers, covering the final layer of lasagne sheets with the remaining béchamel sauce.

5 Sprinkle over the remaining cheese and bake in a preheated oven, 190°C/375°F/Gas Mark 5, for 40 minutes, or until the sauce is golden brown and bubbling. Serve with a green salad, a tomato salad or a bowl of black olives.

beef & pasta bake

serves four

900g/2 lb steak, cubed

150 ml/5 fl oz beef stock

450g/1 lb dried macaroni

300 ml/10 fl oz double cream

½ tsp garam masala

salt

KORMA PASTE

55 g/2 oz blanched almonds

6 garlic cloves

1½ tsp chopped fresh root ginger

6 tbsp beef stock

1 tsp ground cardamom

4 cloves, crushed

1 tsp cinnamon

2 large onions, chopped

1 tsp coriander seeds

2 tsp ground cumin seeds

pinch of cayenne pepper

6 tbsp sunflower oil

TO GARNISH

fresh coriander

flaked almonds

1 To make the korma paste, grind the blanched almonds finely using a pestle and mortar. Put the ground almonds and the rest of the korma paste ingredients into a food processor and process to a very smooth paste.

2 Put the steak in a shallow dish and spoon over the korma paste, turning the steak to coat thoroughly. Leave the meat in the refrigerator to marinate for 6 hours.

3 Transfer the steak and korma paste to a large saucepan, and simmer over a low heat, adding a little beef stock if required, for 35 minutes.

4 Meanwhile, bring a large saucepan of lightly salted water to the boil. Add the macaroni, bring back to the boil and cook for 8–10 minutes, until tender but still firm to the bite. Drain the pasta thoroughly and transfer to a deep casserole. Add the steak, cream and garam masala.

5 Bake in a preheated oven, 200°C/400°F/Gas Mark 6, for 30 minutes until the steak is tender. Remove from the oven and leave to stand for 10 minutes. Garnish with coriander and almonds and serve hot.

neopolitan veal cutlets

serves four

200 g/7 oz butter

4 veal cutlets, about 250 g/9 oz
  each, trimmed

1 large onion, sliced

2 apples, peeled, cored and sliced

175 g/6 oz button mushrooms

1 tbsp chopped fresh tarragon

8 black peppercorns

1 tbsp sesame seeds

2 large beef tomatoes, cut in half

leaves of 1 fresh basil sprig

400 g/14 oz dried marille pasta

100 ml/3½ fl oz extra virgin
  olive oil

175 g/6 oz mascarpone cheese

salt and pepper

fresh basil leaves, to garnish

1 Melt 55 g/2 oz of the butter in a
frying pan. Add the veal and cook
over a low heat for 5 minutes on each
side. Transfer to a dish and keep warm.

2 Add the onion and apples to the
frying pan and cook over a low
heat, stirring occasionally, for 5–8
minutes, until lightly browned. Transfer
to an ovenproof dish, place the veal on
top and keep warm.

3 Melt all but 1 tablespoon of the
remaining butter in the frying pan.
Add the mushrooms, tarragon and
peppercorns. Cook over a low heat for
3 minutes. Stir in the sesame seeds and
transfer to a bowl with the pan juices.
Set aside. Add the tomatoes and basil
to the pan with the remaining butter,
cook for 2–3 minutes and set aside.

4 Bring a large saucepan of salted
water to the boil. Add the pasta
and 1 tablespoon of the oil, bring back
to the boil and cook for 8–10 minutes,
or until tender but still firm to the bite.

Drain and transfer to an ovenproof
dish. Dot with the mascarpone and
sprinkle with the remaining olive oil.

5 Place the onions, apples and veal
on top of the pasta. Spoon the
mushroom mixture on to the cutlets
with the pan juices, place the tomato
halves around the edge and bake in a
preheated oven, 150°C/300°F/
Gas Mark 2, for 5 minutes.

6 Remove from the oven and
transfer to serving plates. Season,
garnish with basil and serve.

Vegetarian & Vegan

Anyone who ever thought that vegetarian meals were dull will be proved wrong by the rich variety of dishes in this chapter. You'll  recognize influences from Middle Eastern and Italian cooking, such as the Stuffed Vegetables, Roasted Pepper Bread, and Sun-dried Tomato Loaf, but there are also traditional recipes such as Pineapple Upside-down Cake and Fruit Crumble. They all make exciting treats at any time of year and for virtually any occasion. Don't be afraid to substitute your own personal favourite ingredients wherever appropriate.

spicy black-eyed beans

serves four

350 g/12 oz dried black-eyed
   beans, soaked overnight in
   cold water

1 tbsp vegetable oil

2 onions, chopped

1 tbsp clear honey

2 tbsp treacle

4 tbsp dark soy sauce

1 tsp mustard powder

4 tbsp tomato purée

450 ml/16 fl oz Vegetable Stock
   (see page 7)

1 bay leaf

1 each fresh rosemary, thyme
   and sage sprigs

1 small orange

1 tbsp cornflour

2 red peppers, deseeded and diced
pepper

2 tbsp chopped fresh flat-leaved
   parsley, to garnish

crusty bread, to serve

1 Rinse the black-eyed beans and place in a saucepan. Cover with water, bring to the boil and boil rapidly for 10 minutes. Drain the beans and place in a casserole.

2 Meanwhile, heat the oil in a large frying pan. Add the onions and cook over a low heat, stirring occasionally, for 5 minutes. Stir in the honey, treacle, soy sauce, mustard and tomato purée. Pour in the stock, bring to the boil and pour over the beans.

3 Tie the bay leaf and herbs together with a clean piece of string and add to the bean mixture in the casserole. Pare off 3 pieces of orange rind using a vegetable peeler and mix into the beans, with plenty of pepper. Cover and cook in a preheated oven, 150°C/300°F/Gas Mark 2, for 1 hour.

4 Squeeze the juice from the orange and blend with the cornflour to form a smooth paste. Stir into the beans with the red peppers. Cover the casserole and return to the oven for 1 hour, until the sauce is rich and thick and the beans are tender. Remove and discard the herbs and orange rind.

5 Garnish with flat-leaved parsley and serve with crusty bread.

pasta & bean casserole

225 g/8 oz dried haricot beans,
    soaked overnight and drained

6 tbsp olive oil

2 large onions, sliced

2 garlic cloves, chopped

2 bay leaves

1 tsp dried oregano

1 tsp dried thyme

5 tbsp red wine

2 tbsp tomato purée

850 ml/1½ pints Vegetable Stock
    (see page 7)

225 g/8 oz dried penne, or other
    short pasta shapes

2 celery sticks, sliced

1 fennel bulb, sliced

125 g/4½ oz mushrooms, sliced

225 g/8 oz tomatoes, sliced

1 tsp dark muscovado sugar

50 g/1¾ oz dried white breadcrumbs

salt and pepper

TO SERVE

salad leaves

crusty bread

1 Place the beans in a saucepan, cover with water and bring to the boil. Boil rapidly for 20 minutes, then drain.

2 Place the beans in a large flameproof casserole, stir in 5 tablespoons of the olive oil, the onions, garlic, bay leaves, herbs, wine and tomato purée and pour in the vegetable stock.

3 Bring to the boil, then cover the casserole and bake in a preheated oven, 180°C/350°F/Gas Mark 4, for 2 hours.

4 Towards the end of the cooking time, bring a large saucepan of lightly salted water to the boil, add the pasta and 1 tablespoon of the oil, and cook for 3 minutes. Drain and set aside.

5 Remove the casserole from the oven and add the pasta, celery, fennel, mushrooms and tomatoes and season to taste with salt and pepper.

6 Stir in the sugar and sprinkle over the breadcrumbs. Cover the casserole again, return to the oven and continue cooking for 1 hour. Serve hot with salad leaves and crusty bread.

mushroom cannelloni

serves four

350 g/12 oz chestnut mushrooms

1 onion, chopped finely

1 garlic clove, crushed

1 tbsp chopped fresh thyme

½ tsp ground nutmeg

4 tbsp dry white wine

50g/1¾ oz fresh white breadcrumbs

12 dried 'quick-cook'
cannelloni tubes

salt and pepper

Parmesan shavings, to garnish

TOMATO SAUCE

1 large red pepper

200 ml/7 fl oz dry white wine

450 ml/16 fl oz passata

2 tbsp tomato purée

2 bay leaves

1 tsp caster sugar

1 Finely chop the mushrooms and place in a saucepan with the onion and garlic. Stir in the thyme, nutmeg and wine. Bring to the boil, cover and simmer for 10 minutes.

2 Add the breadcrumbs, stir to bind the mixture together and season to taste. Remove from the heat and leave to cool for 10 minutes.

3 To make the tomato sauce, halve and deseed the pepper, place on a grill rack under a preheated hot grill and cook for 8–10 minutes, until charred. Leave to cool for 10 minutes.

4 When the pepper has cooled, peel off the charred skin. Chop the flesh and place in a food processor with the wine. Process until smooth, and pour into a saucepan.

5 Add the remaining sauce ingredients to the pepper purée and stir. Bring to the boil and simmer for 10 minutes. Discard the bay leaves.

6 Cover the base of an ovenproof dish with a thin layer of tomato sauce. Fill the cannelloni with the mushroom mixture and place in the dish. Spoon over the remaining sauce, cover with foil and bake in a preheated oven, 200°C/400°F/Gas Mark 6, for 35–40 minutes. Garnish with Parmesan shavings and serve hot.

stuffed vegetables

serves four

4 large beef tomatoes

4 courgettes

2 orange peppers

salt and pepper

FILLING

225 g/8 oz cracked wheat

¼ cucumber

1 red onion

2 tbsp lemon juice

2 tbsp chopped fresh coriander

2 tbsp chopped fresh mint

1 tbsp olive oil

2 tsp cumin seeds

salt and pepper

TO SERVE

warm pitta bread

hummus

COOK'S TIP

It is a good idea to blanch
vegetables (except for tomatoes)
before stuffing. Blanch peppers,
courgettes and aubergines
for 5 minutes.

1 Slice the tops off the tomatoes and reserve, then scoop out the flesh. If the tomatoes will not stand up, cut a thin slice off the bottoms. Chop the flesh and place in a bowl. Season the tomato shells, then invert them on kitchen paper and set aside.

2 Trim the courgettes and cut a V-shaped groove lengthways down each one. Finely chop the cut-out wedges of flesh and add to the tomato flesh. Season the courgette shells to taste and set aside. Halve the peppers, cutting carefully though the stalks. Cut out the seeds and discard, leaving the stalks intact. Season the pepper shells to taste and set aside.

3 To make the filling, soak the cracked wheat according to the instructions on the packet. Finely chop the cucumber and add to the reserved tomato and courgette mixture. Finely chop the red onion and add to the vegetable mixture with the lemon juice, herbs, olive oil, cumin seeds and seasoning and mix together well.

4 When the wheat has soaked, mix with the vegetables and stuff into the tomato, courgette and pepper shells. Place the tops on the tomatoes, transfer to a roasting tin and bake in a preheated oven, 200°C/400°F/Gas Mark 6, for 20–25 minutes, until cooked through. Drain and serve hot or warm with pitta bread and hummus.

lentil & red pepper flan

serves six

PASTRY

225 g/8 oz plain wholemeal flour,
 plus extra for dusting

100 g/3½ oz vegan
 margarine, diced

4 tbsp water

FILLING

175 g/6 oz red lentils, rinsed

300 ml/10 fl oz Vegetable Stock
 (see page 7)

1 tbsp vegan margarine

1 onion, chopped

2 red peppers, deseeded and diced

1 tsp yeast extract

1 tbsp tomato purée

3 tbsp chopped fresh parsley

pepper

1 To make the pastry, sieve the flour into a mixing bowl and add any bran remaining in the sieve. Add the margarine and rub in with your fingertips until the mixture resembles fine breadcrumbs. Stir in the water and bring together to form a dough. Wrap in clingfilm and chill in the refrigerator for 30 minutes.

2 Meanwhile, to make the filling, put the lentils in a saucepan with the stock, bring to the boil, then simmer for 10 minutes, until the lentils are tender. Remove from the heat and mash the lentils into a purée.

3 Melt the margarine in a small frying pan over a low heat, add the onion and red peppers and cook for about 3 minutes, until just soft.

4 Add the lentil purée, yeast extract, tomato purée and parsley. Season to taste with pepper. Mix until thoroughly blended.

5 Roll out the dough on a lightly floured work surface and use it to line a 24-cm/9½-inch loose-bottomed quiche or flan tin. Prick the base of the pastry with a fork and spoon the lentil mixture into the pastry case.

6 Bake in a preheated oven, 200°C/400°F/Gas Mark 6, for 30 minutes, until the filling is set.

brazil nut & mushroom pie

serves four

PASTRY

225 g/8 oz plain wholemeal flour,
plus extra for dusting

100 g/3½ oz vegan
margarine, diced

4 tbsp water

soya milk, to glaze

FILLING

2 tbsp vegan margarine

1 onion, chopped

1 garlic clove, chopped finely

125 g/4½ oz button
mushrooms, sliced

1 tbsp plain flour

150 ml/5 fl oz Vegetable Stock
(see page 7)

1 tbsp tomato purée

175 g/6 oz Brazil nuts, chopped

75 g/2¾ oz fresh
wholemeal breadcrumbs

2 tbsp chopped fresh parsley

½ tsp pepper

1 To make the pastry, sieve the flour into a mixing bowl and add any bran remaining in the sieve. Add the margarine and rub in with your fingertips until the mixture resembles fine breadcrumbs. Stir in the water and bring together to form a dough. Wrap in clingfilm and chill in the refrigerator for 30 minutes.

2 Meanwhile, to make the filling, melt half of the margarine in a frying pan over a low heat. Add the onion, garlic and mushrooms and cook for 5 minutes, until softened. Add the flour and cook for 1 minute, stirring constantly. Gradually add the stock, stirring, until the sauce is smooth and starting to thicken. Stir in the tomato purée, Brazil nuts, breadcrumbs, parsley and pepper. Remove the frying pan from the heat and leave to cool slightly.

3 Roll out two-thirds of the pastry on a lightly floured work surface and use it to line a 20-cm/8-inch loose-bottomed quiche or flan tin. Spread the filling in the pastry case. Brush the edges of the pastry with soya milk. Roll out the remaining pastry to fit the top of the pie. Press the edges to seal, then make a slit in the top of the pastry to allow steam to escape during cooking, and brush with soya milk.

4 Bake in a preheated oven, 200°C/400°F/Gas Mark 6, for 30–40 minutes, until golden brown.

241

roasted pepper bread

serves four

1 tbsp vegan margarine,
   for greasing
1 red pepper, halved and deseeded
1 yellow pepper, halved
   and deseeded
2 fresh rosemary sprigs
1 tbsp olive oil
10 g/¼ oz dried yeast
1 tsp granulated sugar
300 ml/10 fl oz hand-hot water
450 g/1 lb strong white flour
1 tsp salt

1 Grease a 23-cm/9-inch deep round cake tin with margarine.

2 Place the pepper halves and rosemary in a shallow roasting tin. Pour over the oil and roast in a preheated oven, t 200°C/400°F/Gas Mark 6, for 20 minutes, or until slightly charred. Leave the peppers to cool slightly, then remove the skins and cut the flesh into slices.

3 Place the yeast and sugar in a bowl and mix with 100 ml/ 3½ fl oz of hand-hot water. Leave in a warm place for about 15 minutes, or until frothy.

4 Mix the flour and salt together in a large bowl. Stir in the yeast mixture and the remaining water and bring together to form a dough.

5 Knead the dough for 5 minutes, until smooth. Cover with oiled clingfilm and leave to rise for about 30 minutes, or until doubled in size.

6 Cut the dough into 3 equal portions. Roll the portions into rounds slightly larger than the cake tin.

7 Place 1 round in the base of the tin so that it reaches up the sides by about 2 cm/¾ inch. Top with half of the pepper mixture. Strip the leaves from the rosemary sprigs and sprinkle half of them over the top.

8 Place the second round of dough on top, followed by the remaining pepper mixture and rosemary leaves. Place the last round of dough on top. Push the edges of the dough down the sides of the tin.

9 Cover with oiled clingfilm and leave to rise for 30–40 minutes. Bake for 45 minutes, until golden. When the loaf is cooked it should sound hollow when tapped. Turn on to a wire rack. Serve warm.

garlic & sage bread

serves six

1 tbsp vegan margarine,
    for greasing
250 g/9 oz strong brown
    bread flour
1 sachet easy-blend dried yeast
3 tbsp chopped fresh sage
2 tsp sea salt
3 garlic cloves, chopped finely
1 tsp clear honey
150 ml/5 fl oz hand-hot water

1 Grease a baking tray with the margarine. Sieve the flour into a large mixing bowl and add any bran remaining in the sieve.

2 Stir in the dried yeast, chopped sage and half of the sea salt. Reserve 1 teaspoon of the chopped garlic for sprinkling and stir the remainder into the bowl. Add the honey and water and bring together to form a dough.

3 Turn the dough out on to a lightly floured work surface and knead it for about 5 minutes. Alternatively, use an electric mixer with a dough hook.

4 Place the dough in a greased bowl, cover and leave to rise in a warm place until doubled in size.

5 Knead the dough for a few minutes to knock it back, shape it into a ring (see Cook's Tip) and place on the baking tray.

6 Cover and leave to rise for a further 30 minutes, or until springy to the touch. Sprinkle with the rest of the sea salt and garlic.

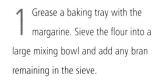

7 Bake the loaf in a preheated oven, 200°C/400°F/Gas Mark 6, for 25–30 minutes. Transfer to a wire rack to cool before serving.

COOK'S TIP

Roll the dough into a long
sausage and then curve it into
a circular shape. You can omit
the sea salt for sprinkling,
if you wish.

sun-dried tomato loaf

serves four

10 g/¼ oz dried yeast

1 tsp granulated sugar

300 ml/10 fl oz hand-hot water

450 g/1 lb strong white flour, plus
  extra for dusting

1 tsp salt

2 tsp dried basil

2 tbsp sun-dried tomato paste or
  tomato purée

1 tbsp vegan margarine,
  for greasing

12 sun-dried tomatoes in oil,
  drained and cut into strips

1 Place the yeast and sugar in a bowl. Mix with 100 ml/3½ fl oz of the water. Leave in a warm place for about 15 minutes, or until frothy.

2 Mix the flour and salt together in a large bowl. Make a well in the dry ingredients and add the basil, yeast mixture, tomato paste and half of the remaining water. Draw the flour into the liquid with a wooden spoon and bring together to form a dough, adding the rest of the water a little at a time.

3 Turn the dough out on to a lightly floured work surface and knead for 5 minutes, or until smooth. Cover with oiled clingfilm and leave in a warm place to rise for about 30 minutes, or until doubled in size.

4 Lightly grease a 900-g/2-lb loaf tin with the margarine.

5 Turn the dough out and knead in the sun-dried tomatoes. Knead for a further 2–3 minutes.

6 Place the dough in the prepared loaf tin and leave to rise for 30–40 minutes. or until doubled in size again. Bake the loaf in a preheated oven, 190°C/375°F/Gas Mark 5, for 30–35 minutes, or until golden. When the loaf is cooked, it should sound hollow when tapped on the base. Cool slightly on a wire rack and serve.

eggless sponge

serves eight

1 tbsp vegan margarine,
   for greasing

225 g/8 oz wholemeal
   self-raising flour

2 tsp baking powder

175 g/6 oz caster sugar

6 tbsp sunflower oil

250 ml/9 fl oz water

1 tsp vanilla essence

4 tbsp strawberry or raspberry
   reduced-sugar spread

caster sugar, for dusting

COOK'S TIP

Standard margarine – packets
that are not labelled vegan –
may contain some animal
products, such as whey, butter
fat or skimmed milk.

1 Grease 2 sandwich cake tins
20-cm/8-inches wide and line the
bases with baking paper.

2 Sieve the flour and baking
powder into a large mixing bowl
and add any bran remaining in the
sieve. Stir in the sugar.

3 Pour in the oil, water and vanilla
essence. Stir with a wooden
spoon for about 1 minute, until the
mixture is smooth, then divide
between the prepared tins.

4 Bake in a preheated oven,
180°C/350°F/Gas Mark 4, for
25–30 minutes, until firm to the touch.

5 Leave the sponges to cool in the
tins, then turn out and transfer
to a wire rack. Carefully remove the
baking paper.

VARIATION

To make a chocolate-flavoured
sponge, replace 15 g/½ oz
of the flour with sieved cocoa
powder. To make a citrus-
flavoured sponge, add the
grated rind of ½ a lemon or
orange to the flour in step 2.
To make a coffee-flavoured
sponge, replace 2 teaspoons
of the flour with instant
coffee powder.

6 Place one of the cooled sponges
on a serving plate. Cover the
surface with the fruit spread, spreading
it out to the edges, and place the other
sponge lightly on top.

7 Lightly dust the eggless sponge
cake with a little caster sugar
before serving.

baked cheesecake

serves six

4 tbsp vegan margarine, melted,
  plus extra for greasing
125 g/4½ oz digestive
  biscuits, crushed
50 g/1¾ oz chopped stoned dates
4 tbsp lemon juice
grated rind of 1 lemon
3 tbsp water
350 g/12 oz firm tofu
150 ml/5 fl oz apple juice
1 banana, mashed
1 tsp vanilla essence
1 mango, peeled, stoned
  and chopped

1 Lightly grease an 18-cm/7-inch round loose-bottomed cake tin with margarine.

2 Mix together the digestive biscuit crumbs and melted margarine in a bowl. Press the mixture into the base of the prepared tin.

3 Put the chopped dates, lemon juice, lemon rind and water into a saucepan and bring to the boil. Simmer for 5 minutes, until the dates are soft, then mash the mixture with a fork.

4 Place the mixture in a food processor with the tofu, apple juice, mashed banana and vanilla essence and process until it forms a thick, smooth purée.

5 Pour the purée over the prepared biscuit-crumb base and gently level the surface with a palette knife.

6 Bake in a preheated oven, 180°C/350°F/Gas Mark 4, for 30–40 minutes, until lightly golden. Leave to cool in the tin, then chill thoroughly in the refrigerator.

7 Place the chopped mango in a blender and process until smooth. Serve the fruit purée as a sauce with the cheesecake.

pineapple upside-down cake

serves eight

4 tbsp vegan margarine, diced, plus
    extra for greasing

425 g/15 oz canned unsweetened
    pineapple pieces in fruit juice,
    drained, with the juice reserved

4 tsp cornflour

50 g/1¾ oz soft brown sugar

125 ml/4 fl oz water

grated rind of 1 lemon

SPONGE

3½ tbsp sunflower oil

75 g/2¾ oz soft brown sugar

150 ml/5 fl oz water

150 g/5½ oz plain flour

2 tsp baking powder

1 tsp ground cinnamon

1 Grease a deep 18-cm/7-inch round cake tin with margarine. Mix the juice from the pineapple with the cornflour until it forms a smooth paste. Put the paste in a saucepan with the sugar, margarine and water and stir over a low heat until the sugar has dissolved. Bring to the boil and simmer for 2–3 minutes, until thickened. Leave the pineapple syrup to cool slightly.

2 To make the sponge, place the oil, sugar and water in a saucepan. Heat gently until the sugar has dissolved, but do not let it boil. Remove from the heat and leave to cool. Sift the flour, baking powder and ground cinnamon into a mixing bowl. Pour over the cooled oil and sugar mixture and beat well to form a batter.

3 Place the pineapple pieces and lemon rind in the prepared tin. Pour over 4 tablespoons of pineapple syrup. Spoon the batter on top.

4 Bake in a preheated oven, 180°C/350°F/Gas Mark 4, for 35–40 minutes, until set and a metal skewer inserted into the centre comes out clean. Place a plate over the top and carefully invert. Leave to stand for 5 minutes, then remove the tin. Serve with the remaining syrup.

apricot slices

makes twelve

PASTRY

100 g/3½ oz vegan margarine,
    diced, plus extra for greasing

225 g/8 oz wholemeal flour

50 g/1¾ oz finely ground
    mixed nuts

4 tbsp water

soya milk, to glaze

FILLING

225 g/8 oz dried apricots

grated rind of 1 orange

300 ml/10 fl oz apple juice

1 tsp ground cinnamon

50 g/1¾ oz raisins

COOK'S TIP

These slices will keep in an
airtight container for 3 or 4 days.

---

1 Lightly grease a 23-cm/9-inch square cake tin. To make the pastry, place the flour and nuts in a mixing bowl and rub in the margarine with your fingers until the mixture resembles breadcrumbs. Stir in the water and bring together to form a dough. Wrap in clingfilm and chill in the refrigerator for 30 minutes.

2 To make the filling, place the apricots, orange rind and apple juice in a saucepan and bring to the boil. Simmer for 30 minutes, until the apricots are mushy. Cool slightly, then place in a food processor and process into a purée. Alternatively, press the mixture through a sieve with the back of a spoon. Add the cinnamon and raisins and stir.

3 Remove the pastry from the refrigerator. Divide in half, roll out one half and use it to line the base of the tin. Spread the apricot purée over the top leaving a border around the edges, and brush the edges with water. Roll out the rest of the dough to fit over the top. Place over the purée and press down the edges to seal.

4 Prick the top of the pastry with a fork and brush with the soya milk. Bake in a preheated oven, 200°C/400°F/Gas Mark 6, for 20–25 minutes, until the pastry is golden. Leave to cool slightly before cutting into 12 bars. Serve warm or cold.

date & apricot tart

serves eight

225 g/8 oz plain wholemeal flour,
    plus extra for dusting
50 g/1¾ oz mixed nuts, ground
100 g/3½ oz vegan
    margarine, diced
4 tbsp water
225 g/8 oz dried apricots, chopped
225 g/8 oz chopped stoned dates
425 ml/15 fl oz apple juice
1 tsp ground cinnamon
grated rind of 1 lemon
soya custard, to serve (optional)

1 Place the flour and ground nuts in a mixing bowl and rub in the margarine with your fingertips until the mixture resembles breadcrumbs. Stir in the water and bring together to form a dough. Wrap the dough in clingfilm and chill in the refrigerator for 30 minutes.

2 Meanwhile, place the apricots and dates in a saucepan with the apple juice, cinnamon and lemon rind. Bring to the boil, cover and simmer over a low heat for about 15 minutes, until the fruit softens. Mash the mixture into a purée and set aside.

3 Remove the pastry from the refrigerator. Reserve a small ball of pastry for making lattice strips. Roll out the remaining dough into a round on a lightly floured work surface and use it to line a 23-cm/9-inch loose-bottomed quiche or flan tin.

4 Spread the date and apricot purée evenly over the base of the pastry case. Roll out the reserved pastry on a lightly floured surface and cut into strips 1 cm/½ inch wide. Cut the strips to fit the tart and gently twist them

across the top of the fruit to form a decorative lattice pattern. Moisten the edges of the strips with water and press the ends firmly against the rim of the tart to seal.

5 Bake in a preheated oven, 200°/400°F/Gas Mark 6, for 25–30 minutes, until golden brown. Cut into slices and serve immediately with soya custard, if you wish.

fruit crumble

serves six

1 tbsp vegan margarine,
  for greasing

6 dessert pears, peeled

1 tbsp chopped stem ginger

1 tbsp dark muscovado sugar

2 tbsp orange juice

CRUMBLE TOPPING

175 g/6 oz plain flour

75 g/2¾ oz vegan margarine, diced

25 g/1 oz almonds, flaked

25 g/1 oz rolled oats

50 g/1¾ oz dark muscovado sugar

soya custard, to serve (optional)

VARIATION

Stir 1 tsp ground mixed spice into
the crumble mixture in step 3 for
added flavour, if you wish.

---

1 Lightly grease a 1-litre/1¾-pint ovenproof dish with the vegan margarine.

2 Core, quarter and slice the pears. Place the pear slices, ginger, muscovado sugar and orange juice in a large bowl and stir to mix well. Spoon the mixture evenly across the base of the prepared dish.

3 To make the crumble topping, sieve the flour into a large mixing bowl. Add the margarine and rub in with your fingertips until the mixture resembles fine breadcrumbs. Add the flaked almonds, then the rolled oats and muscovado sugar, and mix together with your fingers until well blended.

4 Sprinkle the crumble topping evenly over the pear and ginger mixture in the dish.

5 Bake in a preheated oven, 190°C/375°F/Gas Mark 5, for 30 minutes, until the topping is golden and the fruit tender. Serve with soya custard, if you wish.

INDEX